Cooking with Steam

Cooking
with Steam

Spectacular Full-Flavored Low-Fat Dishes

from Your Electric Steamer

Stephanie Lyness

Hearst Books • New York

Library of Congress Cataloging-in-Publication Data
Lyness, Stephanie.
    Cooking with steam: spectacular full-flavored low-fat dishes from
your electric steamer/Stephanie Lyness.
        p.   cm.
    Includes index.
ISBN 0-688-13814-4
1. Steaming (Cookery)   2. Electric food steamers.   I. Title.
TX691.L96 1995
641.7'3—dc20   95-2328
                                                          CIP

Printed in the United States of America

First Edition

1   2   3   4   5   6   7   8   9   10

BOOK DESIGN BY LINEY LI

In memory of the late Jacques Manière,
whose genius led me to the surprising possibilities
of steam

Acknowledgments

I'd like to thank my editor, Ann Bramson, who once again partnered me with her enthusiasm, her vision, and her precious phone time. Brian Buckley and Lisa Trolund cheerfully survived a long summer testing and developing recipes in my un-air-conditioned kitchen; Brian contributed much of his personal cooking repertoire to this book. Judith Sutton edited the manuscript with intelligence and grace. And thanks to my mentor, Barbara Kafka, whose work with me over the past several years made this book a pleasure to write.

Thanks to my neighborhood merchants on the Upper West Side of Manhattan who have, and do, support my work with their friendship and respect—Bill Bowers and his staff at Jake's Fish Market, Harry Oppenheimer and his staff at Oppenheimer Co., and Michel and Eleanor Guiton and their staff at the Broadway Butcher.

Thanks to friends in the food world who listened to me talk about yet another steaming book: Dona Abramson, Katherine Alford, Pam Anderson, Gail Arnold, Jack Bishop, Mark Bittman (particularly for his expertise on greens), Marion Gorman, Paul Grimes, Judy Hill, Chris Kimball at Cooks Illustrated, Ris Lacoste, Tina Ujlaki, and Nach Waxman at Kitchen Arts and Letters. Thanks to Shirley Corriher for her tip about lemon zest in vinaigrettes, Bill Russo for his inspiration for apricots with lime as well as his devotion to broccoli rabe, and Kazuto Matsusaka for his recipe for Tomato-Shallot Vinaigrette.

Thanks to Bob and Eleanor Lyness, Cole and Mary Fisher, Eric Wolff, Dick Nodell, Kate Harper, Cathy Schwartzman, and Clint Fisher—family, extended family, and friends who tasted and gently critiqued the food, helping me to hold myself to the task.

And all my love to Joanna.

Contents

Introduction

What Are Electric Steamers and Why Should We Use Them?

Last year, while I was steaming my way through a cookbook on stove-top steaming, a food writer told me with great enthusiasm about her favorite appliance—an electric steamer made by Waring. An electric steamer? I'd never even heard of one. But, being in the business of steaming, I got hold of the Waring and tried it out. It was easy to use and it cooked great-tasting food quickly. But what really spoke to me was the blessedly no-work feel of the machine: I put the food in the steamer, plugged it in, set my timer, and walked away. There was no temperature to gauge, no worry about burning the food, and no surveillance. When the timer rang, dinner was ready—and I hadn't really done *anything*. Even better, there was very little to clean up.

Most of us associate steaming with healthful, if somewhat unglamorous, food. It's true that steaming gives us a way to prepare food with no added fat. It's also been shown that steaming preserves the nutrients in food better than any other cooking technique apart from microwaving. And nutrients in cooked foods are more available to our bodies than those in raw foods. But steamed food doesn't lack for flavor; in fact, the opposite is true. Steaming gives us a chance to taste the essence of the food rather than what's been done to it. Steaming reveals subtle flavors that are often cloaked by fat. And, though I hate to admit it, even as a professional cook I have little desire to spend my limited free time cooking; steaming is fast and easy, and an electric steamer makes steaming even more convenient.

Learning to use an electric steamer is about as demanding as learning to use a blender; a quick peek in the instruction booklet that comes with your steamer gives you most of the information you'll need. The recipes in this book are, for the most part, simple and equally self-explanatory. But benefit from my experience and read the following pages on the different machines—how to choose the best one for you and how to make the most of it—and on how to use the recipes, along with some safety tips.

The Machines

The electric food steamers on the market fall into two categories: All-purpose food steamers with a rice bowl or compartment for steaming rice, and rice cookers with a perforated plate attachment that lets you steam other foods in addition to rice. However, none of the rice cookers I looked at had much room for steaming water under the plate, so I nixed them as impractical for the recipes in this book.

In order to be certain that a given recipe might work in more than one machine, I chose four sturdy food steamers that were large enough to accommodate the foods I like to steam: the Waring Deluxe Steam Cooker #SC–1, the West Bend Steamer #86600, the Rival Automatic Steamer/Rice Cooker #4450, and the large-size Black & Decker Handy Steamer Plus #HS90. Black & Decker also makes a smaller model with half the steaming capacity, but it was too small for my purposes.

All four machines work on the same principle: Water is heated in a reservoir in the base of the machine to create steam. The food steams above the reservoir in a covered perforated steaming basket. All of the machines except the Waring use some type of drip pan to catch the juices from the food so that the juices don't land in the reservoir. The drip pan allows you to make sauces from the collected steaming juices, often without even having to reduce them. All the machines are plastic and all have an automatic turn-off safety feature so that the machine shuts off if the steaming water evaporates. All have a solid-bottomed rice bowl attachment for steaming rice and for steaming foods with liquid.

Despite differences in size, shape, and gadgetry among these four models, variations in actual steaming times and procedures are minimal, and you should be able to make the recipes in this book in most electric steamers. Two of the machines (the Rival and Waring) steam some foods, such as artichokes and corn, a bit faster than the others, but the difference is minor enough to be absorbed in the normal range of cooking times allowed for in a recipe. There is occasionally a difference in method for the particular machines when making sauces, because the Waring has no drip pan. Check the Equipment Notes at the end of each recipe for any major variations in timing or procedure among the machines. If you do use another machine, just as with any piece of cooking equipment, once you're familiar with the machine you'll be able to adjust the recipes where necessary.

Which machine is right for you? It's really a matter of personal preference. If your counter space is limited, you may prefer a compact round machine, such as the Black & Decker, over the larger oval Rival. An oval shape may be more convenient if you will be steaming a lot of fish fillets. I particularly like the machines with timers that double as on/off switches because I'd rather not have to unplug the machine to turn it off; maybe you don't care. If you like to flavor foods by steaming over a flavored liquid, choose the Waring or the Black & Decker; I prefer to flavor foods by steaming them directly on a bed of herbs and to use the juices in the drip pan for sauces rather than reducing the steaming liquid. The suggested retail prices for these machines range from $40 to $70.

BLACK & DECKER HANDY STEAMER PLUS #HS90

This machine has a white plastic base and a four-quart clear plastic round steaming basket. The clear plastic makes it easy to see how the food is doing as it steams; when the bowl steams up, a sharp tap on the lid clears it momentarily. The lid and the eight-cup rice bowl are also made of clear plastic. The lid can be overturned and used as as base on which to set the steaming basket after the food is cooked, to catch drips, or when serving directly from the basket. The machine is easy to clean and all the parts except the base are dishwasher-safe.

The seventy-five-minute timer built into the base acts as an on/off switch; the machine starts heating when the timer is engaged and turns off when the timer runs out or is turned to the off position. (The timer must be turned past the ten-minute mark to start the machine.) A small red indicator light next to the timer lights up when the machine is heating—a handy reminder since the timer will work even if the machine is unplugged.

The drip pan is a deep doughnut-shaped attachment that fits under the steaming basket and holds up to four cups of liquid. A large drip pan like this one is useful because you don't have to worry about it over-flowing when steaming foods that give off a lot of liquid, such as clams, chicken, or ribs. Liquids such as chicken broth or wine and other flavoring ingredients such as herbs and spices can be added to the steaming water. The unit includes a separate divider bowl attachment that fits into the steaming basket to separate food in the basket, but I've never found it necessary.

This is the cheapest of the four steamers.

RIVAL AUTOMATIC STEAMER/RICE COOKER

The Rival is an oval machine with a shallow seven- by eleven-inch black plastic steaming basket. The basket has two "ears" for easy removal from the base. The clear plastic lid is domed to a height of three and a half inches, so the steamer holds more than you'd think by looking at the basket; the lid has a knob on the top to pick it up. The oval rice bowl holds seven cups. All of the parts except the base are dishwasher-safe (top rack only); the instruction booklet notes that prolonged dish-washing can fade the printing on the various parts.

The lid fits more tightly than on the other models I tested; this may be the reason the Rival steams some foods a bit more speedily than some other steamers. The oval basket is convenient for steaming longer items, such as fish fillets and asparagus.

The Rival has neither a timer nor an on/off switch; a red indicator light goes on when it's plugged in and starts heating. In lieu of a timer, the instruction booklet suggests using a measured amount of water in the reservoir as a timer—the machine turns off automatically when the water runs out—and, to this end, includes a chart of minutes of steam per amount of water. While this system can work, I find it more practical to use a kitchen timer, given the normal variation in steaming times for food.

The water reservoir is divided into two parts: an outer reservoir that acts as the drip pan and an inner reservoir with heating element to heat the water. This machine takes only water, with no flavorings. The steaming holes are placed around the outside edge of the steaming basket so the steaming juices drip into the outer reservoir/drip pan. To collect these juices, you must either boil the water in the inner reservoir away before pouring the juices out or use a bulb baster to collect them.

This machine requires more counter space than the Black & Decker because it's oval. The steaming basket on my machine isn't quite level, so steamed custards don't come out level. And over time the lid has warped, so that it's difficult to get it on and off the base.

The inside of the inner reservoir must be scrubbed with ordinary white vinegar after each use. I did this pretty faithfully, but still got what the booklet accurately describes as a "tea kettle whistle" during steaming, the fate of those who don't clean well enough.

This machine costs between $40 and $50.

WARING DELUXE STEAM COOKER #SC6-1

The Waring is a very sturdy oval machine with a black plastic base and two thick-walled stackable white steaming baskets with flat "ears" on either side that act as handles. Additional baskets can be ordered from Waring; the instruction booklet suggests steaming with no more than three baskets at a time. This is one of the more expensive machines. It weighs about twice what the other machines weigh. One of the baskets holds about six quarts of food. The second is divided by a center wall (with a hole in the center for the steam) into two compartments: One half is solid, for steaming rice and foods with sauces; the other half has one small steam hole. The lid is flattish, with "ears" on either side that cover the basket handles. The lid can be overturned to act as a base on which to set the basket after steaming, to catch drips, or when serving directly from the basket. The baskets and lid are dishwasher-safe (top rack only).

The great advantage of this machine is that, because it has two stackable compartments, you can steam a whole meal in one go: fish, meat, or chicken in the large bottom basket, rice and a vegetable in the top. The recipes in this book don't take advantage of this feature because none of the other steamers has the same capability, but don't let this stop you from experimenting. You can cook rice with and steam over any liquid you like (wine, beer, stock, etc.) in this machine.

Like the Rival, the Waring has neither an on/off switch nor a timer. The entire lid, including the handles, gets very hot during steaming. The handles are tricky to grasp because they don't extend beyond those on the basket.

Because this machine does not have a drip pan, the steaming basket sits in the reservoir, very near the level of the steaming water. When steaming fish, the juices cause the water to bubble up into the steaming basket, so be sure to use as little water as possible in the reservoir (up to the Low line), or the fish will poach rather than steam. Start with very little water when steaming chicken as well; the chicken gives off juices faster than the water evaporates, so that in no time the juices will have risen high enough to bubble into the steaming basket.

WEST BEND STEAMER

The West Bend is an oval machine with a ten-cup clear plastic steaming basket and a clear plastic lid. The lid can be overturned to use as a platter under the steamer basket, to catch drips, or when serving directly from the basket. The drip pan is a shallow oval insert that fits into the base, with a center handle for lifting. The rice bowl holds six cups. This is the lightest machine of the four. It's also one of the more expensive.

A sixty-minute timer is built into the base (the timer must be turned past the fifteen-minute mark to start the machine heating) and a red indicator light lights up to show that the machine is heating. Only water can be used in the reservoir. All parts of this steamer except the base are dishwasher-safe (top rack only).

This machine has features similar to the Black & Decker: a timer that does double duty as an on/off switch, a clear plastic basket that lets you see how the food is doing, and a lid that's easy to remove. The drip pan is small: Be sure to empty it midway during steaming when cooking foods that give off a lot of juice, such as shellfish, poultry, and ribs. Because the drip pan has only one center handle instead of two on either end, a full pan may tip when you lift it out of the machine; it's best to check and empty the pan when it's only half-full, so you don't lose any juices or burn yourself with any that slop over the side.

Steaming with Stackable Steamers

The great advantage of steaming with a double-tiered steamer like the Waring is that it offers the opportunity to steam more than one dish at a time in the same machine. Steamed rice is a fast, easy, and healthy accompaniment to many of the recipes in this book: Try steaming it in the upper compartment while Red Snapper with Lemon and Ginger (page 64), Cod with Bell Peppers and Tomato (page 66), Soy-Orange–Marinated Chicken Cutlets (page 93), or Chicken Breasts Stuffed Under the Skin with Rosemary Butter (page 97) steam underneath. Rice steamed along with Scallops Marco Polo (page 80) makes a meal for two, complete with starch and vegetable. It's just as easy to steam a vegetable while a main course cooks, such as plain steamed potatoes along with Swordfish with Anchovy Mayonnaise (page 74) or Monkfish with Black Pepper–Mustard Sauce (page 75); or try Ratatouille (page 47) with Cornish Game Hens Stuffed with Provençal Herbs (page 102). Or steam a custard for dessert in the compartment above Kasha-Stuffed Turkey Cutlets with Zucchini (page 107) or Beef Shin "Pot-au-Feu" (page 116).

Steaming two dishes at once is a matter of simple common sense. Start the dish with the longer steaming time first and add the more quickly cooking food to the upper compartment. Be aware, however, that juices from the food in the upper compartment will drip down into the lower compartment: As a rule, therefore, I steam fish below other foods regardless of timing, unless the other food is steamed covered, as is a custard. Be aware as well that some foods take slightly longer to steam in the upper compartment than in the lower.

The Recipes

These recipes were developed specifically for electric steamers; steaming times for stove-top steamers are different. I use my electric steamer as just one of the tools in my kitchen. Steaming gives a particular clean, bright flavor no other cooking method can match. It's a terrific way to cook an astonishingly broad range of foods, and I have found steaming to be the very best way to cook some foods (such as artichokes). But I don't steam indiscriminately, and I don't believe that anyone should.

These recipes use only those foods that truly benefit from steaming, for reasons of flavor or texture and/or to reduce fat. Where possible, these recipes are low in fat, but many are not; I won't sacrifice flavor for low-fat ingredients. You'll find three recipes for different kinds of ribs because I jump up and down each time I see how beautifully the steamer renders their fat, leaving the ribs moist and succulent. And you'll find lots of different custards in the dessert chapter; the steamer is far easier to use than the traditional water bath. There are a lot of fish recipes, because steamed fish is divine (and doesn't smell up my house). Almost all of these recipes are cooked exclusively in the steamer; a few, like Apple-Cinnamon Bread Pudding, use it in addition to the stove top or oven.

Steaming in these machines is so straightforward that for some ingredients you almost don't need a recipe. To that end, I've included charts of steaming times for a variety of vegetables and fish, as well as for rice, the most likely candidates for a quick steamed meal, so you can steam a simple meal without even having to look at a recipe.

Many of the recipes, particularly those for fish and chicken, are for two servings rather than four because, with some exceptions, seafood and chicken parts must be steamed in a single layer to cook evenly, and electric steamers aren't big enough to steam for four. For custards, I could squeeze three but not four custard cups into the steamers. Some custards, such as Coconut Rice Pudding, are made in the rice bowl and do serve four, but others are so much more attractive in individual dishes that I opted for the custard cups for two. You can always double the recipe and steam the custards in two batches if need be. For some rich desserts, such as the Bittersweet Chocolate Pudding Cake, I used four-ounce aluminum cupcake cups made by EZ-Foil; four of these fit easily in all the steamers.

Each recipe tells you the appropriate amount of water to put in the reservoir—Low, Medium, or High. All the steamer reservoirs are marked with lines to indicate water level: The Black & Decker and the Waring have markings for Low, Medium, and High, the West Bend has Minimum and Maximum markings, and the Rival has five different levels. *Use the Minimum mark on the West Bend when the recipe calls for either Low or Medium water levels. On the Rival, use the second line from the bottom for Low, the next line up for Medium, and the top line for High.*

Whenever possible, recipes call for starting food in a cold steamer, because that's the easiest thing to do. Green vegetables, however, require a preheated steamer, in which the water is already boiling, or the vegetables will lose their vibrant green color. Where preheating is necessary, the charts and recipes call for preheating the steamer at the top of the page.

If you need to open the steamer to check on the food or add something, do so quickly to minimize loss of steam and temperature. Add a minute or so to the steaming time for every time you take the lid off.

Safety

Steam is very hot: Assume that all parts of the machine are hot when in use. Use oven mitts when opening the lid of the steamer, and open the lid away from you to let the steam escape before putting your hands or face into or over the steamer basket. Turn off the steamer before you open the lid. During steaming, be careful of the steam that escapes from under the lid; if using the Rival, be especially careful of the single hole in the lid that vents the steam—the lid fits tightly, so the steam shoots out from the hole. Don't use the steamers under overhanging cabinets, because the steam can damage them.

Vegetables

V egetables are a natural choice for steaming, a method that preserves their nutrients and brings to the fore their subtle and often delicate flavors. Steaming makes cooking vegetables easy. It's faster than blanching, because you don't need to bring a large pot of water to the boil, and once cooked, the vegetables can be drained in the steaming basket itself in the sink.

You don't really need a recipe to steam vegetables for everyday meals: Steamed vegetables are tasty enough to be eaten plain or with melted butter or olive oil, salt and pepper, and maybe a squeeze of lemon. The chart of Steaming Times for Vegetables on page 14 gives steaming times so you can do just that, and many of the recipes in this chapter are hardly more complicated. But as steaming does such a special thing for vegetables, it's sometimes worth giving them our full attention and serving them on their own as either a first course or a light meal. With a little added accompaniment or two (cheese for the panzanella-stuffed artichokes, hummus and bread with the tabbouleh variation, bread and perhaps a salad with the shrimp stuffing), three of the artichoke recipes, for example, are substantial enough for a light meal. Steamed asparagus is so delicate that it begs to be enjoyed on its own as a first course. Steamed celery has a unique flavor and, while it can be served as a side dish with roasted poultry or meat, once in a while it deserves center stage. On the other hand, saucy vegetable dishes such as Ratatouille, Cabbage in a Bacon Cream Sauce, and Marinated Bell Peppers can double as sauces for plain steamed fish or poultry.

Green vegetables are traditionally blanched in boiling water, while root vegetables are started in cold water. This same rule applies when steaming—that is, green vegetables must be steamed in a preheated steamer to preserve their color. Longer-cooking vegetables such as artichokes, carrots, and potatoes are fine started in a cold steamer. When necessary, the chart and the recipes call for preheating the steamer before adding the vegetables: Put the required amount of water in the base, add the drip pan (if there is one) and the covered steaming basket, and heat until the water is boiling and you can see steam escaping from under the lid. Then add the vegetables to the basket, cover, and begin timing. If there is no indication to preheat, just put the vegetables in the steaming basket as usual, turn the steamer on, and start timing.

If you'd like to serve the vegetables cold, steam them and then set the basket in the sink under cold running water to refresh them. Drain the vegetables in the basket.

Don't salt vegetables during steaming; the salt just washes off. Salt and pepper them, if you like, before serving.

STEAMING TIMES FOR VEGETABLES

◆ **Quantities are for four unless otherwise specified. See individual vegetable recipes for more detailed information on how to cut and trim vegetables.**

◆ **Water level is Medium unless otherwise noted.**

◆ **Preheat the steamer (bring the water to a boil in the base before adding the vegetable) where noted; otherwise, steaming water is cold from the tap.**

Artichokes (Water Level: High)

4 medium to large (½ to ¾ pound):

Prepare as on page 19 and steam upside down until the base is tender, 35 to 45 minutes.
• **Equipment Notes:** If using the West Bend, buy ½-pound or smaller artichokes and steam for 30 to 35 minutes; the basket isn't large enough to hold 4 large artichokes.

Asparagus   Preheat the Steamer

1 bunch (about 1⅓ pounds) medium stalks, stalks trimmed:

Steam until the stalks give when pressed between two fingers, about 8 minutes. Toss once during steaming to get the ones on the bottom up to the top.

Green Beans   Preheat the Steamer

1 pound, ends trimmed:

Steam until tender, about 12 minutes.

Beets   (Water Level: High)

1¼ pounds, rinsed but unpeeled, and stems, if any, trimmed to 1 inch:

Steam until very tender: small (about 2 inches in diameter), about 30 minutes; medium (about 3 inches in diameter), about 40 minutes. Let cool, then peel and slice or cut up.

Broccoli   Preheat the Steamer

1 bunch (about 1 pound), stems trimmed, tops cut into florets, and stalks (which can be trimmed with a knife to cut off the tough outer peel) cut on the diagonal into ¼-inch slices:

Steam until bright green and just tender, 6 to 8 minutes.

Broccoli Rabe   Preheat the Steamer

1 bunch (about 1¼ pounds), stems trimmed, top flowery parts cut into 3-inch-long pieces, and stems cut into 1-inch segments (about 5 cups):

Steam tops and stems together until tender, about 10 minutes.
• **Equipment Notes:** Although 5 cups broccoli rabe looks like too much to fit into the Rival and the West Bend machines, it does: It settles as it cooks.

Green Cabbage

½ large head, quartered, cored, and cut lengthwise into ½-inch-wide strips (10 cups strips):

Steam until wilted but not mushy, about 10 minutes.
• **Equipment Notes:** The Black & Decker holds up to 10 cups, the Waring 8 cups, the Rival and West Bend only 5 cups; 8 to 10 cups serves 4, 4 to 5 cups serves 2. (If steaming for 4 in the Rival or West Bend, steam the cabbage in two batches.) The steaming time is still 10 minutes for the maximum quantity in all machines except for the Rival—it takes only about 8 minutes.

Carrots

1 pound peeled baby or mini carrots:

Steam until tender, about 20 minutes.

Standard carrots, peeled and sliced on the diagonal ⅛ to ¼ inch thick:

Steam until tender, 18 to 20 minutes.

Cauliflower

One 1¾-pound head, cored and cut into florets (serves 4 to 6):

Steam until tender, 13 to 15 minutes.

Celery

1 celery heart, stalks separated, trimmed, peeled deeply with a knife, and cut on the diagonal into 1½- to 2-inch-long pieces:

Steam until tender, 15 to 20 minutes.

Corn

4 ears, husked:

Steam until tender, 8 to 10 minutes.
• **Equipment Notes:** The Rival and Waring steam in 8 minutes; the other two steamers need 10 minutes.

4 ears, wrapped in foil with butter (see page 37):

Steam until tender, about 25 minutes (turn the ears over once during steaming).

Cucumbers   Preheat the Steamer

2 cucumbers, peeled, halved lengthwise, and seeds scraped out with a spoon, then cut into 2- by ¼-inch strips (see page 38) or ⅛- to ¼-inch half-moons (see page 57):

Steam until tender, about 10 minutes.

Kale

1 bunch, stemmed as for spinach (see Note, page 47) and leaves torn into small pieces or cut into ½-inch-wide strips (6 cups packed stemmed leaves; serves 2 generously):

Steam until tender, about 15 minutes. Stir once during cooking.
• **Equipment Notes:** All the steamers except the Rival hold 6 cups raw kale; it holds 4 cups, enough for 2 small servings.

Potatoes (Waxy)   (Water Level: High)

1 pound small potatoes (about 2 ounces each, 2 to 3 inches long), unpeeled:

Steam until very tender: whole, about 35 minutes; quartered, 25 to 30 minutes.

Spinach   Preheat the Steamer

1 large head (1 to 1¼ pounds) smooth- or crinkly-leaved, about 6 cups packed (cooks down to about 1 cup, enough to serve 2), stemmed (see Note, page 47):

Steam until wilted, about 10 minutes. Stir halfway through the steaming time:
• **Equipment Notes:** All the steamers except the Rival hold 6 cups raw spinach; it holds 4 cups, enough for 2 small servings. If steaming for 4 in the Rival, steam the spinach in two batches.

Snow Peas   Preheat the Steamer

1 pound, trimmed and stringed if necessary:

Steam until the color brightens, about 5 minutes.

Sugar Snap Peas   Preheat the Steamer

1 pound, trimmed and stringed if necessary:

Steam until the color brightens, about 5 minutes.

Swiss Chard

1 large head (6 cups packed leaves), stemmed as for spinach (see page 47):

Steam until tender, about 10 minutes. Stir halfway through the steaming.

• **Equipment Notes:** All the steamers except the Rival hold 6 cups raw chard; the Rival holds 4 cups, enough for 2 small servings. (Or steam the larger amount in two batches.)

Zucchini   Preheat the Steamer

1¼ pounds, trimmed and cut crosswise on the diagonal ¼ inch thick:

Steam until tender, about 10 minutes.

Steamed Artichokes

Serves 4
Water Level: High

Steamed artichokes are truly wonderful eaten on their own with no sauce at all, but a little vinaigrette or butter sauce doesn't hurt. Serve Lemon Butter Sauce with hot or warm artichokes, Mustard Vinaigrette with warm or cold artichokes.

4 medium ($^1/_2$- to $^3/_4$-pound) artichokes (see Equipment Notes)
$^1/_2$ lemon
Lemon Butter Sauce (page 83; triple the recipe) or Mustard Vinaigrette (page 20)

Cut the stems off the artichokes close to the bases so they stand upright. Lay the artichokes on their sides and cut off the top third of each one. Rub the cut surfaces with the lemon half as you work. Cut off the sharp tips of the remaining leaves with kitchen scissors and place the artichokes stem ends up in the steaming basket in a single layer. Cover and steam until the stem ends are tender when pierced with a small knife, 35 to 45 minutes.

Remove the steaming basket to a plate on the sink and let the artichokes stand until cool enough to handle.

Pull out the small purplish leaves that cover the chokes. Scrape out the furry chokes with a small spoon.

Serve the artichokes warm or at room temperature with the butter sauce, or cold or at room temperature with the vinaigrette.

Set the artichokes upright on individual plates and pour the sauce or vinaigrette into the centers.

Mustard Vinaigrette

Makes 1 scant cup

1 tablespoon Dijon mustard
2 tablespoons fresh lemon juice
1 tablespoon water
¹⁄₄ teaspoon salt
¹⁄₈ teaspoon freshly ground black pepper
¹⁄₂ cup plus 2 tablespoons olive oil

In a medium bowl, whisk the mustard with the lemon juice, water, salt, and pepper. Whisk in the olive oil in a thin stream, slowly at first until the vinaigrette emulsifies, and then more quickly.

• **Equipment Notes:** If using the West Bend, buy ¹⁄₂-pound or smaller artichokes and steam for 30 to 35 minutes; the basket isn't large enough to hold 4 larger artichokes.

Panzanella-Stuffed Artichokes

Serves 4
Water Level: High

This is a somewhat more elaborate way to prepare artichokes. The panzanella, or bread salad, soaks the artichokes in the vinaigrette, saturating them with flavor. The artichokes are superb the day they're made and at least as good, or even better, the next. Accompanied by a chunk of cheese and a plate of Marinated Bell Peppers (page 30), they make a meal.

This recipe is easily cut in half if you're cooking for two.

4 medium (¹/₂- to ³/₄-pound) artichokes (see Equipment Notes)
¹/₂ lemon

<u>PANZANELLA</u>
2 cups firmly packed torn-up white bread, such as Italian bread
 or baguette, with crust
2 medium ripe tomatoes (1 pound total)
1 medium garlic clove, minced
¹/₄ cup plus 2 tablespoons olive oil
¹/₄ cup red or white wine vinegar
2 tablespoons chopped flat-leaf parsley
¹/₄ teaspoon salt
¹/₄ teaspoon freshly ground black pepper

Cut the stems off the artichokes close to the bases so they stand upright. Lay the artichokes on their sides and cut off the top third of each one. Rub the cut surfaces with the lemon as you work. Cut off the sharp tips of the remaining leaves with kitchen scissors and place the artichokes stem ends up in the steaming basket in a single layer. Cover and steam until the bases of the artichokes are tender when pierced with a small knife, 35 to 45 minutes.

Meanwhile, combine all the ingredients for the panzanella in a medium bowl. Taste and adjust the seasoning.

Leaving the artichokes in the steaming basket, refresh them under cold running water. Drain well. Pull out the small purplish leaves that cover the chokes. Scrape out the furry chokes with a small spoon.

Divide the panzanella among the artichokes, spooning it into the cavities in the center and then stuffing the remainder between the leaves. Serve immediately, or cover and refrigerate until chilled, or overnight.

VARIATION

Artichokes Stuffed with Tabbouleh

Prepare, steam, refresh, and clean four artichokes as directed in the recipe above. Make the tabbouleh while the artichokes steam. Stuff the artichokes with the tabbouleh, as directed in the recipe above. Cover and refrigerate until cold, about 2 hours.

$3/4$ **cup medium-crack bulgur**
2 cups boiling water
$1^1/2$ **cups chopped ripe tomatoes**
$1/4$ **cup olive oil**
2 tablespoons fresh lemon juice
$1/2$ **cup chopped flat-leaf parsley**
$1/4$ **cup chopped fresh mint**
$3/4$ **teaspoon salt**
$1/4$ **teaspoon freshly ground black pepper**

Put the bulgur in a bowl and pour the boiling water over. Let stand until the bulgur is tender but still has some bite, about 45 minutes. Drain well.

Mix the bulgur with the remaining ingredients.

• **Equipment Notes:** If using the West Bend, buy $1/2$-pound or smaller artichokes and steam for 30 to 35 minutes; the basket isn't large enough to hold 4 larger artichokes.

Artichokes Stuffed with Shrimp

Serves 4

Water Level: High

The mayonnaise that sauces the shrimp stuffing is very mildly flavored with anchovy, adding richness more than a decidedly anchovy taste. If you're dead set against anchovies, however, you needn't add them at all—the dish is good without them.

1 pound small shrimp (31 to 35 count), peeled and deveined
4 medium ($^1/_2$- to $^3/_4$-pound) artichokes (see Equipment Notes)
$^1/_2$ lemon

ANCHOVY MAYONNAISE

2 anchovy fillets packed in oil
1 medium garlic clove, chopped
$^1/_3$ cup mayonnaise, homemade (page 24) or store-bought regular
   or low-fat
1 tablespoon fresh lemon juice
1 tablespoon chopped flat-leaf parsley
2 dashes of Tabasco sauce

Arrange the shrimp in a single layer in the steaming basket, cover, and steam until the shrimp turn pink and are cooked through, 8 to 12 minutes (see Equipment Notes). Remove them from the steaming basket and let cool.

Trim, steam, refresh, and clean the artichokes as directed on page 19.

Meanwhile, for the mayonnaise, using a mortar and pestle, mash the anchovies and garlic to a paste. Or mash on a cutting board, using the flat side of a large knife. Put the paste in a bowl and stir in the remaining ingredients.

Roughly chop the shrimp and stir them into the mayonnaise.

Stuff the artichokes with the shrimp mixture as directed on page 20 and refrigerate until chilled, about 2 hours.

continued

• **Equipment Notes:** If using the West Bend, buy ½-pound or smaller artichokes and steam for 30 to 35 minutes; the basket isn't large enough to hold 4 larger artichokes.

If using the Waring, use the shorter steaming time for the shrimp.

Mayonnaise

Makes about 1 cup

1 large egg yolk
1 teaspoon Dijon mustard
1 tablespoon fresh lemon juice or vinegar, or more to taste
½ teaspoon salt, or more to taste
¾ cup vegetable or olive oil, or a combination of the two
Freshly ground black pepper

Whisk together the egg, mustard, lemon juice, and salt in a medium bowl. Whisk in the oil in a thin stream, slowly at first until the mayonnaise emulsifies, and then a bit more rapidly. Add pepper to taste and taste for salt. Add more lemon juice or vinegar if you like. Serve immediately, or press plastic wrap onto the surface of the mayonnaise and refrigerate for up to 2 days.

Asparagus with Lemon Oil

Serves 4

Water Level: Medium

Preheat the Steamer

I often finish hot steamed vegetables with a simple lemon vinaigrette, but if I'm not serving them immediately the acid in lemon juice and vinegars turns green vegetables gray. I borrowed the idea for this recipe from Shirley Corriher, a food scientist who seems to be able to speak with authority and genuine enthusiasm on any topic having to do with food or cooking. She uses lemon zest rather than the juice, thereby adding flavor without acid so the vegetables stay green. You can drizzle this oil on any hot or cold vegetable, including those that aren't green, but I'm particularly fond of it with asparagus.

If you want to make the oil in quantity, go ahead; it lasts for several weeks in the refrigerator.

LEMON OIL

Grated zest of 1 lemon
2 tablespoons olive oil

1 to 1⅓ pounds medium asparagus, stalks trimmed
Salt and freshly ground black pepper

For the lemon oil, stir together the zest and oil. Let stand while you steam the asparagus.

Preheat the steamer. Pile the asparagus in the steaming basket, cover, and steam, tossing halfway through the steaming so that the spears cook evenly, until just tender, about 8 minutes. Remove the steaming basket and shake well over the sink to drain. Pat the asparagus dry with paper towels and put it on a serving plate. Drizzle the oil over and sprinkle with salt and pepper. Serve hot, cold, or at room temperature.

Green Beans with Lemon

Serves 4
Water Level: Medium
Preheat the Steamer

This is a dead-simple preparation that I use for any green vegetable, particularly beans, asparagus, and zucchini. Add the oil, lemon, salt, and pepper just before serving so the acid in the lemon juice doesn't turn the beans gray.

1¼ pounds green beans, trimmed
1 tablespoon olive oil
1 tablespoon fresh lemon juice, or to taste
⅛ teaspoon salt
Freshly ground black pepper

Preheat the steamer. Pile the beans in the steaming basket, cover, and steam until bright green and tender, 12 to 14 minutes. Remove the steaming basket and shake well over the sink to drain.

Put the beans in a serving bowl. Just before serving, add the oil, lemon juice, salt, and pepper and toss. Serve hot, cold, or at room temperature.

Green Beans with Walnuts and Sherry Vinegar

Serves 4

Water Level: Medium

Preheat the Steamer

Serve this hot as a side dish or cold as a salad or first course. The walnuts add flavor and crunch, but don't pass up the recipe if you don't have any on hand. I steam green beans past "crisp-tender" because a longer-cooked bean has better flavor. Add the vinaigrette just before serving so the beans hold their bright green color.

¼ cup chopped walnuts

SHERRY VINAIGRETTE

1 small shallot, chopped
2 teaspoons sherry vinegar
¼ teaspoon salt
⅛ teaspoon freshly ground black pepper
2 tablespoons olive oil
1 tablespoon chopped flat-leaf parsley

1¼ pounds green beans, trimmed

Preheat the oven to 425°F.

Spread the walnuts on a baking sheet and toast in the oven until fragrant, 7 to 10 minutes. Let cool.

For the vinaigrette, whisk together the shallot, vinegar, salt, and pepper in a large bowl. Whisk in the oil and parsley. Set aside.

Preheat the steamer. Pile the beans in the steaming basket, cover, and steam until bright green and tender, 12 to 14 minutes. If serving cold, leaving the beans in the steaming basket, refresh under cold running water. Drain and pat dry on paper towels. Add the beans to the vinaigrette and toss to coat.

Beet Salad with Oranges and Nut Oil

Serves 4
Water Level: High

Make this salad with a navel orange, if possible; it's easy to slice and nicer to serve because it has no seeds. Nut oils are available at specialty food stores. They vary in strength: My brand, À l'Olivier, is quite strong, so I cut it with olive oil. If your oil isn't particularly strong, just use two tablespoons nut oil and omit the olive oil.

1¼ pounds beets, preferably small to medium (2 to 3 inches in diameter), stems trimmed to 1 inch and rinsed

ORANGE VINAIGRETTE
1 medium navel orange, zest grated and reserved
2 teaspoons sherry vinegar
⅛ teaspoon salt
Pinch of freshly ground black pepper
1 tablespoon walnut or hazelnut oil
1 tablespoon olive oil (see headnote)
1 tablespoon chopped flat-leaf parsley

Put the beets in the steaming basket, cover, and steam until very tender when pierced with a small knife, 30 to 40 minutes, depending on size. Remove from the steamer and let stand until cool enough to handle. Using a small knife, peel and trim the beets. Cut them into ¼-inch-thick slices and cut the slices into ¼- to ⅓-inch-thick strips.

For the vinaigrette, whisk together the orange zest, vinegar, salt, and pepper in a medium bowl. Whisk in the oils and then the parsley. Add the beets and toss gently to coat.

Just before serving, set the orange on end and cut off all of the skin and the bitter white pith with a very sharp knife or a serving knife. Turn the orange on its side and cut into thin slices, then cut the slices in half. Overlap the slices on a serving plate to make a ring. Mound the beets in the center.

Beets with Yogurt, Sour Cream, and Chives

Serves 4
Water Level: High

Serve this very cold, like borscht, as a salad or vegetable side dish. It rounds out a meal of cold chicken or fish; it's particularly good with salmon.

1¼ pounds beets, preferably small to medium (2 to 3 inches in
diameter), stems trimmed to 1 inch and rinsed
¼ cup low-fat plain yogurt
1 tablespoon sour cream
2 teaspoons fresh lemon juice
¼ teaspoon salt
Pinch of freshly ground black pepper
1 tablespoon chopped fresh chives or scallion greens

Put the beets in the steaming basket, cover, and steam until very tender when pierced with a small knife, 30 to 40 minutes, depending on size. Remove from the steamer and let stand until cool enough to handle.

Meanwhile, stir together the yogurt, sour cream, lemon juice, and salt in a medium bowl.

Using a small knife, peel and trim the beets. Cut them into ⅓- to ½-inch-thick slices and cut the slices into ⅓- to ½-inch-thick strips. Add to the yogurt mixture and toss gently to mix. Refrigerate until very cold, 2 to 3 hours. Just before serving, taste the beets for salt and pepper (you'll probably need to add some). Sprinkle with the chives or scallion greens and serve cold.

Marinated Bell Peppers

Serves 2 to 3
Water Level: Medium

In this recipe, bell peppers are peeled and marinated, as in any of the myriad recipes for marinated roasted peppers. The difference is in the steaming: Steamed marinated peppers have a more delicate taste than roasted, because roasting adds a smoky flavor that steaming does not. I've always used red and yellow peppers in this recipe, not because the green aren't tasty, but because they're more difficult to peel.

Serve the peppers as a vegetable side dish, or with goat or feta cheese in a sandwich; pour the flavored oil over the bread.

2 red bell peppers, halved, cored, seeded, and ribs removed
2 yellow bell peppers, halved, cored, seeded, and ribs removed
1 tablespoon balsamic vinegar
¼ cup olive oil
4 to 6 leaves fresh basil, torn into pieces
½ teaspoon chopped fresh thyme or ¼ teaspoon dried, crushed
⅛ teaspoon freshly ground black pepper

Put the pepper halves in the steaming basket, cover, and steam for 25 to 30 minutes (see Equipment Notes). Remove from the steamer and let stand until cool enough to handle.

Peel off the pepper skins with your fingers. Tear the peppers lengthwise into strips an inch or so wide (they tear naturally along the visible lines in the flesh), and put them in a shallow baking dish or gratin dish. Add the remaining ingredients and toss to coat the peppers. Cover and refrigerate overnight.

• **Equipment Notes:** Steam the peppers for 25 minutes in the Waring and Rival machines, 30 minutes in the other machines.

Broccoli Rabe with Rosemary Oil and Pine Nuts

Serves 4

Water Level: Medium

Preheat the Steamer

Rosemary Oil is easy to make and keeps for several weeks in the refrigerator, so I usually have it on hand for this recipe. If you don't, you can just use more olive oil.

To my taste, broccoli rabe must be cooked a bit more than broccoli, until it is really tender and loses its bright green color.

2 tablespoons pine nuts
Salt
1 large bunch (1¼ pounds) broccoli rabe
1 teaspoon Rosemary Oil (page 63)
1 teaspoon olive oil
Freshly ground black pepper

Preheat the oven to 400°F.

Spread the pine nuts on a baking sheet and toast them in the oven until golden brown, 5 to 7 minutes. Be careful—once they start to brown, they can burn quickly. Dump them onto a paper towel–lined plate, salt them lightly, and set aside.

Cut the flowery tops of the broccoli rabe into 3-inch lengths. Then cut the remaining stems into 1-inch pieces.

Pile the broccoli rabe in the steaming basket, cover, and steam until it is tender and has just lost its bright green color, about 10 minutes. Remove the steaming basket and shake well over the sink to drain.

Put the broccoli rabe in a serving bowl, add the oils and salt and pepper to taste, and toss. Sprinkle with the pine nuts and serve hot or at room temperature.

Brian's Penne with Broccoli and Garlic

Serves 2
Water Level: Medium
Preheat the Steamer

This pasta is dressed with only a whisper of a sauce—garlic-infused olive oil and butter with a splash of chicken stock to extend it. The recipe is also delicious made with broccoli rabe or steamed greens such as kale or Swiss chard (see the chart on page 14 for steaming times). When I'm in a hurry, I don't bother with the parsley or Parmesan cheese; they dress up the dish but aren't critical to its success. If you're not overly concerned about fat, add a second tablespoon of butter.

1 tablespoon butter
2 tablespoons olive oil
4 garlic cloves, slivered
¼ cup chicken stock or canned low-sodium broth, poultry steaming
**   liquid, or water**
Salt
½ pound penne
2 to 4 tablespoons freshly grated Parmesan cheese (optional)
1 large or 2 small stalks broccoli, stems trimmed, tops cut into florets,
**   stems peeled deeply with a small knife and cut crosswise on the**
**   diagonal into ¼-inch slices (3 generous cups)**
1 tablespoon chopped flat-leaf parsley (optional)
Freshly ground black pepper

Bring a large pot of water to a boil for the penne. Preheat the steamer.

Meanwhile, melt the butter with the oil in a large frying pan over medium heat. Add the garlic and cook until fragrant and just beginning to turn golden, 1 to 2 minutes. Add the stock and remove from the heat.

Salt the pasta water heavily (it should taste salty), add the penne, and cook until al dente, about 9 minutes. Drain and put into a large bowl. Toss with the cheese, if using.

Meanwhile, put the broccoli in the steaming basket, cover, and steam until bright green but still crisp, about 6 minutes. Remove the steaming basket and shake well over the sink to drain. Add the broccoli to the pan with the garlic mixture.

When the pasta is almost cooked, bring the stock in the frying pan to a boil over high heat, stirring to coat the broccoli.

Add the broccoli mixture and the parsley, if using, to the bowl with the pasta and toss to coat the pasta with the sauce. Season to taste with pepper and serve immediately.

Carrots with Lemon and Cilantro

Serves 4
Water Level: Medium

The combination of lemon and cilantro brings out the sweetness of the carrots. If you prefer to cook the carrots in advance you can heat the butter in a large frying pan, add the carrots and salt, and toss until lightly browned and hot. Add the remaining ingredients off the heat.

1 to 1¼ pounds carrots, peeled and cut crosswise on the diagonal into ⅛- to ¼-inch-thick slices
1 tablespoon butter, at room temperature
1 teaspoon fresh lemon juice
1 teaspoon chopped fresh coriander
1 teaspoon chopped flat-leaf parsley
¼ teaspoon salt
⅛ teaspoon freshly ground black pepper

Put the carrots in the steaming basket, cover, and steam until tender, 18 to 20 minutes. Remove the steaming basket and shake well over the sink to drain.

Put the carrots in a serving bowl, add the remaining ingredients, and toss gently to mix. Serve hot.

Cabbage in Bacon Cream Sauce

Serves 4
Water Level: Medium

This recipe is a variation on one in Jacques Manière's *Cuisine à la Vapeur*. The steamer renders some of the fat from the bacon before it is added to the cream sauce. I like to use this as a bed for plain steamed chicken, fish, or pork tenderloin; the creamy cabbage serves as a sauce.

4 slices bacon, cut into 1-inch-wide pieces
$1/2$ large head green cabbage, quartered, cored, and cut lengthwise into
  $1/2$-inch-wide strips (about 10 cups strips; see Equipment Notes)
$1/4$ cup plus 2 tablespoons light or heavy (whipping) cream
$1^1/2$ tablespoons chopped flat-leaf parsley
$1/2$ teaspoon salt
Freshly ground black pepper

Put the bacon in the steaming basket, cover, and steam for 15 minutes. Transfer to a large frying pan and set aside.

Add the cabbage to the steaming basket, cover, and steam until wilted but not mushy, about 10 minutes. Remove the steaming basket to a plate or the sink and let drain.

Add the cream, parsley, and salt to the frying pan with the bacon, and bring to a boil over medium-high heat. Add the cabbage and pepper to taste and cook, tossing the cabbage for about 2 minutes until the cabbage is heated through and the cream has reduced to coat it. Serve hot.

• **Equipment Notes:** The Rival and West Bend machines won't hold 10 cups cabbage strips; cook the cabbage in two batches if using those machines. For the Waring, you can cut the cabbage to 8 cups (it holds that amount comfortably), and leave the other quantities as is (or cook the 10 cups cabbage in two batches).

Brian's Cauliflower

Serves 4 to 6
Water Level: Medium

My friend Brian, whose recipe this is, told me that although he doesn't really care for cauliflower, he does like it prepared this way. I like cauliflower, and I'm crazy about his recipe. One tablespoon of butter is enough but two tablespoons is even better. Carrots are delicious cooked this way as well. This is quite spicy; you may want to start with an eighth of a teaspoon red pepper flakes.

1 head (about 1³/₄ pounds) cauliflower, cored and cut into florets
1 tablespoon butter
2 tablespoons olive oil
¹/₄ teaspoon salt
1 tablespoon chopped flat-leaf parsley
¹/₄ teaspoon hot red pepper flakes, or to taste

Put the cauliflower florets in the steaming basket, cover, and steam until just tender, 13 to 15 minutes. Remove the steaming basket and shake well over the sink to drain.

Melt the butter with the oil in a large frying pan over high heat. Add the cauliflower and salt and cook, stirring frequently, until the cauliflower turns a light golden brown, about 5 minutes. Add the parsley and red pepper flakes and cook, stirring, for about 30 seconds. Serve hot.

Celery with Olive Oil, Lemon, and Parmesan

Serves 2

Water Level: Medium

Steamed celery may sound weird, but try it anyway. Steaming mellows the sharp taste of the raw vegetable so that it tastes almost like its knobby relative, celery root. Steamed celery gains flavor if cooled to room temperature, and it makes an unusual first course or addition to an antipasto platter.

When steaming celery, use hearts rather than a regular head; even when peeled, large stalks are so stringy that they're unpleasant to eat. (Even the more tender celery hearts must be peeled to remove the strings.)

1 celery heart, stalks separated and trimmed
1 tablespoon olive oil
1 teaspoon fresh lemon juice
Salt and freshly ground black pepper
1 scant tablespoon freshly grated Parmesan cheese

Use a small knife to peel the celery stalks lengthwise to remove the strings, and cut them on the diagonal into 1- to 1½-inch pieces. Put the celery in the steaming basket, cover, and steam until tender, 15 to 20 minutes. Remove the steaming basket and shake well over the sink to drain.

Put the celery in a serving bowl and toss with the oil, lemon juice, and salt and pepper to taste. Sprinkle with the Parmesan cheese. Let cool to room temperature before serving.

Louisiana Crab-Boil Corn

Serves 2

Water Level: Medium

In Louisiana they boil crayfish, crabs, and a variety of vegetables such as corn, potatoes, onions, and artichokes in a broth flavored with something called crab boil seasoning, a mixture of dried herbs and spices. Old Bay Seasoning is a comparable mixture that is available nationally; traditional Louisiana brands, such as Zatarain's, may be hard to find outside of the region. I discovered that corn slathered with butter flavored with Old Bay and steamed in aluminum foil is delicious. You can use this same technique to steam corn with an herb butter (butter mashed with a fresh or dried herb), such as the Rosemary Butter on page 97.

2 tablespoons butter, at room temperature
1 teaspoon Old Bay Seasoning
Pinch of freshly ground black pepper
2 ears corn, husked

Aluminum foil

In a small bowl, mash the butter with Old Bay seasoning and pepper.

Cut two pieces of aluminum foil about 12 by 10 inches. Set an ear of corn in the center of each and slather with the butter. Wrapping the ears loosely so that there is room in the package for steam, bring the sides of the foil up to meet over the corn and fold over together three times in ¼-inch folds to seal. Fold over the ends the same way.

Place the wrapped corn in the steamer, cover, and steam, turning the ears once, for 25 minutes.

Open the foil packages and transfer the corn to plates. Pour the melted butter that has collected in the packages over the corn and serve hot.

Sautéed Cucumbers

Serves 4
Water Level: Medium
Preheat the Steamer

Cooked cucumbers are an oddity to Americans but very common in France, where they are blanched and then they're sautéed in butter. Cooking deepens and sweetens their taste. Their delicate flavor particularly complements steamed fish. If you are pressed for time, just cut the seeded cucumber halves into quarter-inch half-moons instead of into strips.

2 medium cucumbers, peeled
1 tablespoon butter
$\frac{1}{8}$ teaspoon salt
Pinch of freshly ground black pepper

Preheat the steamer. Cut the cucumbers in half lengthwise and use a spoon to scrape out the seeds. Cut each half crosswise into 2-inch sections, and cut each section lengthwise into $\frac{1}{4}$-inch-wide strips.

Put the cucumbers in the steaming basket, cover, and steam for 10 minutes. Leaving the cucumber in the basket, refresh under cold running water. Shake over the sink to drain well, and then pat dry on paper towels.

Heat the butter in a medium frying pan over medium-high heat until foaming. Add the cucumbers, salt, and pepper and cook, stirring, until glazed with butter, about 30 seconds. Serve hot.

Marinated Eggplant

Serves 4 to 6
Water Level: Medium

I use small Italian eggplant (they range in size from about two to about eight ounces) for this dish because they have fewer and smaller seeds than large eggplant. Traditionally eggplant is salted and drained to remove bitterness; I've never tasted a steamed eggplant that was bitter, so I skip that step.

Serve this as you would marinated peppers, as a first course on its own or, with goat or feta cheese, as part of a marinated vegetable platter or in a sandwich.

1¹/₂ pounds small Italian eggplant, trimmed and cut lengthwise
   into ¹/₃-inch-thick slices
¹/₂ teaspoon black peppercorns
¹/₄ cup olive oil
1 tablespoon red wine vinegar
1 small garlic clove, thinly sliced
1 scant tablespoon fresh thyme leaves or ¹/₂ teaspoon dried
1 teaspoon kosher salt

Put the eggplant slices in the steaming basket, sprinkle with the peppercorns, cover, and steam until the eggplant is tender but not falling apart, about 15 minutes. Transfer the eggplant and spices to a medium baking dish. Add the remaining ingredients. Cover and refrigerate. Let marinate overnight, or up to 5 days, turning the eggplant in the marinade occasionally. Let come to room temperature before serving.

Rice

Electric steamers are terrific for cooking rice. It's easier to make rice this way than on top of the stove because you never have to adjust the heat to prevent the water from evaporating before the rice is cooked, and the water doesn't bubble over. In short, it's foolproof. You can steam rice with plain water or stock or with vegetables, herbs, and/or spices for flavoring.

The accompanying chart gives measurements and times for steaming long- or short-grain white and short-grain brown rice in water or stock. Put the rice and the water or stock (you must use boiling liquid for the Waring) in the rice bowl, stir, and set the rice bowl in the steaming basket (if using the Waring or Rival, the bowl sits directly on the base). Cover and steam for the amount of time given in the chart. Then turn off the steamer and let the rice stand, covered, for five minutes before serving.

You can reheat cold leftover rice in the rice bowl in ten to fifteen minutes.

MACHINE	RICE	LIQUID	STEAMING TIME
Black & Decker	1 cup long- or short-grain white	1¼ cups	35 minutes, plus 5 minutes standing time
	1 cup short-grain brown	1½ cups	1 hour, plus 5 minutes standing time
Rival	1 cup long- or short-grain white	1¼ cups	35 minutes, plus 5 minutes standing time.
	1 cup short-grain brown	1½ cups	1 hour, plus 5 minutes standing time
West Bend	1 cup long- or short-grain white	1½ cups	35 minutes, plus 5 minutes standing time
	1 cup short-grain brown	1½ cups	1 hour, plus 5 minutes standing time
Waring	1 cup long- or short-grain white	1½ cups (Boiling)	45 to 50 minutes, plus 5 minutes standing time
	1 cup short-grain brown	1½ cups (Boiling)	1 hour, plus 5 minutes standing time

The following two recipes are for rice with vegetables. The risotto can be made with either long-grain white rice or Arborio rice, which cooks in the same time as white rice. If possible, use homemade stock or the liquid saved from steaming poultry rather than canned broth for these recipes. Not only is the flavor of homemade stock superior to canned, it gives the Arborio rice (if you're lucky enough to find it) the trademark creaminess of risotto.

Rice Pilaf with Peas and Mushrooms

Serves 4
Water Level: High

Use the chart on page 41 to determine the correct quantity of water or stock to use in your machine.

One 10-ounce package frozen petit peas
1 cup long-grain white rice
8 ounces white mushrooms, trimmed and thinly sliced
$^1\!/_4$ cup chopped onion
1 tablespoon butter (optional)
1 bay leaf
$^1\!/_2$ teaspoon chopped fresh thyme or $^1\!/_4$ teaspoon dried
$^1\!/_4$ teaspoon salt
Chicken stock or poultry steaming liquid or a combination of two-thirds
    canned low-sodium broth and one-third water (see Equipment Notes)

Put the peas in the steaming basket, cover, and steam for 10 minutes to thaw. Remove from the steaming basket and set aside.

Put the rice, mushrooms, onion, the butter, if using, the bay leaf, thyme, salt, and the stock or broth mixture in the rice bowl and stir (do not cover with aluminum foil). Place the bowl in the steaming basket, cover, and steam according to the timing in the chart on page 41. Stir in the peas, turn off the steamer, and let stand covered, for 5 minutes.

• **Equipment Notes:** If using the Rival or Waring steamers, put the rice bowl directly on the steamer base, as described in the instruction manuals, rather than in the steaming basket.

Risotto with Porcini Mushrooms

Serves 4 as a side dish or 2 as a main course
Water Level: High

Although I sometimes make this recipe with long-grain rice, the short-grain Arborio rice traditionally used for risotto gives the dish a satisfying chew and creaminess. If you use long-grain rice, refer to the chart on page 41 to find the correct quantity of water or stock to use in your machine. Made with Arborio rice and Parmesan cheese, this dish is rich enough to serve as a main course for two.

I tried this recipe several times with Arborio rice in the Waring and found that I consistently had more success with the other machines. So, if your machine is a Waring, use long-grain rice rather than Arborio, with the quantities and timings on the chart; the finished dish will be more like a pilaf than a risotto.

6 large pieces dried porcini mushrooms ($^1/_4$ to $^1/_3$ ounce)
$^2/_3$ cup boiling water
1 cup Arborio or long-grain white rice (see headnote)
$^1/_4$ cup chopped onion
1 teaspoon chopped fresh thyme or $^1/_4$ teaspoon dried
1$^1/_2$ cups chicken stock or poultry steaming liquid or 1 cup canned low-sodium broth plus $^1/_2$ cup water, for Arborio rice; for long-grain rice, use $^1/_2$ cup less than the quantity given in the chart on page 41 (see Equipment Notes)
$^1/_2$ teaspoon salt
1 tablespoon butter (optional)
Freshly ground black pepper
$^1/_4$ cup freshly grated Parmesan cheese (if serving as a main course)

continued

Put the mushrooms in a small bowl and pour the boiling water over them. Let soak for 30 minutes. Remove the mushrooms and coarsely chop. Strain the soaking liquid through a fine sieve and reserve.

Combine the rice, mushrooms, the reserved soaking liquid, the onion, thyme, stock or broth mixture, the salt, and the butter, if using, in the rice bowl and stir (do not cover with foil). Put the rice bowl in the steaming basket, cover, and steam until the rice is tender but still moist, 35 to 40 minutes, or 45 to 50 minutes if using the Waring. Spoon onto individual serving plates and sprinkle with pepper to taste and the Parmesan cheese if serving as a main course.

• **Equipment Notes:** If using the Rival or Waring steamers, put the rice bowl directly on the steamer base, as described in the instruction manuals, rather than in the steaming basket.

Potatoes with Thyme Butter

Serves 4
Water Level: High

You can make this recipe with small whole (about two ounces) potatoes if you find them (see the chart on page 14 for the steaming time). Otherwise, cut larger potatoes into quarters, sixths, or eighths, depending on their size. Use thyme butter with steamed fish, chicken, and vegetables other than potatoes, as well as with grilled meats.

1¼ pounds waxy potatoes, cut into bite-sized pieces (quarters, sixths, or eighths, depending on size)

THYME BUTTER
2 tablespoons butter, at room temperature
1 teaspoon chopped fresh thyme or ¼ teaspoon dried
Pinch each of salt and freshly ground black pepper

Put the potatoes in the steaming basket, cover, and steam until tender, 25 to 30 minutes.

Meanwhile, in a small bowl, mash together the butter, thyme, and salt and pepper. Taste for seasoning.

When the potatoes are cooked, dump them into a serving bowl, add the butter, and toss to coat. Serve hot.

Sautéed Spinach with Garlic and Lemon

Serves 2
Water Level: Medium
Preheat the Steamer

I owe this recipe to my friend Mark Bittman, an excellent cook and an authority on greens. Use this preparation for any steamed green. Toasted pine nuts (see page 31) are a good addition if you have the time—and the pine nuts.

1¼ pounds spinach, stems trimmed (see Note) and well washed
  (6 to 7 packed cups leaves; see Equipment Notes)
2 tablespoons olive oil
2 medium garlic cloves, minced
⅛ teaspoon salt
Pinch of freshly ground black pepper
1 tablespoon fresh lemon juice, or to taste

Pack the spinach into the steaming basket, cover, and steam, stirring halfway through the steaming time, until wilted, about 10 minutes. Leaving the spinach in the steaming basket, refresh under cold running water. Drain well and squeeze dry in handfuls to get rid of as much water as possible. Coarsely chop.

Heat the oil in a medium frying pan over low heat. Add half the garlic and cook until golden, 1 to 2 minutes. Add the spinach, the remaining garlic, the salt, and pepper and cook, stirring, until the spinach is warmed through and the garlic is fragrant, about 1 minute. Remove from the heat and add the lemon juice. Taste for seasoning and for lemon juice, and serve immediately.

• **Equipment Notes:** The West Bend, Waring, and Black & Decker steamers hold 6 to 7 cups leaves; the Rival holds only 4, so you will need to cook the spinach in batches.

• **Note:** If the spinach leaves are large, fold each leaf in half lengthwise, with the veined side out, and strip off the stem that runs up the leaf. If the leaves are small and the stems thin, just cut off the stems close to the bottom of each leaf.

Ratatouille

Serves 4 to 6
Water Level: Medium

Most recipes for ratatouille call for sautéing each vegetable separately in a luxurious amount of olive oil and then combining all the cooked vegetables. In this vastly simplified low-fat version, the vegetables are steamed together and sautéed in a small amount of oil for flavor. (If you're not concerned about fat, another tablespoon or two of olive oil added to the pan with the tomatoes only makes this dish better.) Steaming makes it unnecessary to salt the eggplant before cooking because steamed eggplant is never bitter. And steamed eggplant absorbs much less oil than raw eggplant, so the dish is less oily.

I use small Italian eggplant because they have fewer and smaller seeds than larger eggplant.

This can be made at least a day ahead; it gets better as it sits.

3 tablespoons olive oil
1 large onion, cut in half through the root end and thinly sliced
   (about 2 cups)
1 teaspoon chopped fresh thyme or $^1/_2$ teaspoon dried
Salt
$^3/_4$ pound small eggplant
$^3/_4$ pound small or medium zucchini
1 medium red bell pepper
1 pound plum tomatoes, cored and chopped, or 1 cup chopped
   canned Italian plum tomatoes
4 garlic cloves, minced
1 tablespoon chopped flat-leaf parsley
$^1/_8$ teaspoon freshly ground black pepper

continued

Heat 2 tablespoons of the oil in a large frying pan over medium-low heat. Add the onion, thyme, and ½ teaspoon salt, cover, and cook slowly until the onions are tender and very sweet, about 20 minutes. Uncover the pan, raise the heat to medium-high and cook, stirring, for about 5 minutes to caramelize the onions to a golden brown color. Remove the onions to a bowl and set the pan aside.

Meanwhile, put the eggplant, zucchini, and bell pepper in the steaming basket, cover, and steam until the vegetables are tender, 15 to 20 minutes. Remove the steaming basket and shake well over the sink to drain.

Heat the remaining 1 tablespoon oil in the frying pan over high heat. Add the steamed vegetables and the tomatoes and cook, stirring gently, until the tomatoes are softened, 4 to 5 minutes. Add the garlic, parsley, ½ teaspoon salt, and the pepper and cook until the garlic is fragrant, about 1 minute. Stir in the onions and taste for seasoning. Serve hot or cold.

Steamed Vegetable Medley

Serves 4

Water Level: Medium

The steamer makes it easy to cook a combination of vegetables. If the vegetables have good flavor, this is tasty enough to be served plain, with just a sprinkling of salt and chopped fresh herbs, if you like, such as tarragon, parsley, or chives. Or add a drizzle of olive oil, butter, Lemon Oil (page 25), or Thyme Butter (page 45), or dress the vegetables with lemon juice and olive oil, as on page 26.

2 medium carrots, peeled and cut on the diagonal into $^1/_4$-inch-thick slices
$^1/_2$ pound green beans, trimmed
$^1/_2$ bunch broccoli (about 8 ounces), stems trimmed, cut into florets,
   stalks peeled deeply with a knife and cut on the diagonal into $^1/_4$-inch-
   thick slices
$^1/_2$ red bell pepper, cored, seeded, ribs removed, and cut into $^1/_4$-inch-
   wide strips
Salt

Put the carrots and beans in the steaming basket, cover, and steam for 10 minutes. Add the broccoli and steam for 5 minutes longer. Add the peppers and steam for 5 more minutes. Dump out into a serving bowl, sprinkle with salt, and serve hot.

Fish and Shellfish

Steaming is a perfect way to cook fish and shellfish because it keeps the delicate flesh from drying out and doesn't get in the way of the clean, endlessly varied taste of fresh seafood. Steamed lean white fish, such as cod, halibut, and snapper, stay moist, and steaming shows off their delicate and refined flavors. Steamed oily fish, such as salmon and bluefish, are buttery and more mild-flavored than one could imagine. Monkfish, a dense-fleshed fish that dries out easily with dry heat, is less tricky to steam than to roast or sauté. Even swordfish, a fish most of us are so used to grilling that we'd never even think of steaming it, has a luscious texture and a completely new flavor when steamed.

Like vegetables, most fresh fish has so much taste that it can just be steamed and eaten with lemon juice, or lemon with melted butter or olive oil. A sprinkling of fresh chopped herbs, scallions, or capers tastes good too. The charts on page 54 and page 56 give steaming times for many common fish, both steaks and fillets, and for shellfish, so you don't even have to consult a recipe.

The fun of cooking fish is that there are so many different kinds. Most of the recipes in this chapter steam the fish plain and then serve it with a simple sauce made on the side. If you can't find a particular fish called for in the recipe, don't hesitate to substitute another similar fish. Lean white fish such as cod, halibut, and snapper can be substituted for one another in the recipes, as can tuna, swordfish, salmon, and bluefish. Use the chart to determine steaming times when substituting. (I haven't given steaming times for flounder—often sold here as sole— because I don't think steaming is the best way to cook it.)

Fish can be steamed in fillet or steak form. I like to steam steaks because the fish has more flavor when cooked on the bone and—particularly so when steaming flaky cod—the flesh holds together better on the bone. With the exception of salmon, a sturdy fillet, most fillets are very delicate once cooked and fall apart easily. It's easiest to steam them on a piece of lightly buttered or oiled aluminum foil so that you can remove the cooked fish from the steamer in one piece by picking up opposite corners of the foil and lifting it out of the basket. The foil also keeps the fish from sticking to the basket.

Steaming fish is easy; the only risk is overcooking, because fish continues to cook even after it leaves the steamer. With the exception of swordfish, the times on the chart are for cooking the fish to medium-rare, with a resting time of two minutes, during which time the fish will cook all the way through. I let the fish rest in the steaming basket, covered, in the sink so that it stays warm and any extra juices that would dilute the sauce can drain away.

Most of the recipes in this chapter are for two because the steaming baskets of the electric machines are just large enough to hold two fillets or steaks, or shellfish for two. Large, wide fillets, like snapper, are best steamed on top of each other because they won't fit neatly side by side in the baskets; the chart gives times for a single fillet as well as for two stacked fillets.

These steamers are terrific for cooking shrimp if you follow one important rule: It must be steamed in a single layer, or it cooks unevenly. If you're steaming a lot of shrimp, line them up like spoons in a drawer, nestled one next to another. If the steamer is filled to the maximum with shrimp, the steaming time will be a few minutes longer than if steaming only a few.

The Waring steamer is a good shape for fish fillets because it's oval. However, if there is too much water in the reservoir, the water bubbles up over the fish so that it poaches more than it steams. Add water just to the Low mark; fish steams quickly and gives off its own liquid, so there's no problem with the water evaporating before the fish is cooked.

I salt fish before steaming but add pepper only after the fish is cooked; steaming doesn't do anything to enhance the flavor of the pepper.

STEAMING FISH FILLETS AND STEAKS

◆ Steaming times are counted from the time the cold steamer is turned on.

◆ Steaming water is cold from the tap.

◆ Water level is Medium (Low if using the Waring).

◆ Steaming times, except for swordfish, are to cook the fish to medium-rare; it will finish cooking all the way through during the two-minute resting time. Steam swordfish to rare so that it ends up medium-rare in the very center; it's tough if over-cooked.

Bluefish fillet (6 to 8 ounces, 3/4 inch thick)

10 to 11 minutes, plus 2 minutes standing time

Catfish fillet (6 to 8 ounces, 3/4 inch thick)

13 to 14 minutes, plus 2 minutes standing time

Cod fillet (6 to 8 ounces, 3/4 inch thick)

11 to 12 minutes, plus 2 minutes standing time

Cod steak (8 to 10 ounces, 3/4 to 1 inch thick)

15 minutes, plus 2 minutes standing time

Halibut steak (8 to 10 ounces, 3/4 to 1 inch thick)

15 minutes, plus 2 minutes standing time

Monkfish fillet (1 inch thick at thickest point)

15 minutes, plus 2 minutes standing time

Red Snapper fillet (about 6 ounces)

Single fillet (6 to 8 ounces, $1/2$ inch thick): 9 to 10 minutes, plus 2 minutes standing time

Two stacked fillets: 17 to 20 minutes, plus 2 minutes standing time

Salmon fillet (6 to 8 ounces, $1^1/4$ inches thick)

18 to 20 minutes, plus 2 minutes standing time

Salmon steak (8 to 10 ounces, 1 inch thick)

11 to 13 minutes, plus 2 minutes standing time

Swordfish steak (6 to 8 ounces, 1 inch thick)

12 to 14 minutes, plus 2 minutes standing time (see headnote)

Tuna steak (6 to 8 ounces, $3/4$ to 1 inch thick)

15 minutes, plus 2 minutes standing time

STEAMING SHELLFISH

- ◆ Steaming times are counted from the time the cold steamer is turned on.
- ◆ Steaming water is cold from the tap.
- ◆ Water level is Medium (Low if using the Waring).

Littleneck Clams (1 to 2 pounds)

Steam until open, 15 to 20 minutes.

Lobster Tails (4 ounces)

Frozen: 20 minutes
Thawed: 10 to 12 minutes

(8 to 10 ounces)

Frozen: 25 to 30 minutes
Thawed: 17 minutes

Mussels (1 to 2 pounds)

Steam until open, about 15 minutes

Sea Scallops Medium (about ½ to 1 inch thick)

8 to 10 minutes

Large (about 1½ inches thick)

12 to 15 minutes

Shrimp Small (26 to 35 count)

8 to 12 minutes, depending on quantity

Medium (16 to 25 count)

10 to 14 minutes, depending on quantity

Cold Steamed Salmon with Cucumber-Yogurt Sauce

Serves 2

Water Level: Medium (Low if using the Waring)

It's much easier to steam salmon than to poach it; you don't have to make a poaching liquid, and steaming is less messy. And the salmon loses none of its flavor to a poaching liquid. Both the salmon and the sauce can be made hours ahead.

**2 salmon fillets (6 to 8 ounces each), about 1¼ inches thick at the
    thickest point**
Salt
**1 medium cucumber, peeled, halved lengthwise, seeds scraped out
    with a spoon, and cut into ⅛ to ¼-inch-thick half-moons**
½ cup low-fat plain yogurt
1 tablespoon rice wine vinegar or white wine vinegar
1 scallion, thinly sliced
1 teaspoon chopped fresh dill
⅛ teaspoon freshly ground black pepper

Place the salmon fillets, skin side down, in a single layer in the steaming basket. Sprinkle with salt, cover, and steam until salmon is just barely cooked through but still translucent in the very center, 18 to 20 minutes. Use a spatula to transfer the salmon to a plate, and let cool while you make the sauce. Rinse out the steaming basket.

For the sauce, put the cucumber in the steaming basket, cover, and steam until translucent, about 10 minutes. Leaving the cucumber in the basket, refresh under cold running water. Drain well, then pat dry with paper towels.

Stir together the yogurt, vinegar, scallion, dill, ¼ teaspoon salt, and the pepper in a small bowl. Gently fold in the cucumber.

Cover both the salmon and sauce and refrigerate until completely chilled, at least 2 hours. Serve the salmon with the sauce.

Salmon with Kazuto's Tomato-Shallot Vinaigrette

Serves 2
Water Level: Medium (or Low if using the Waring)

This vinaigrette is adapted from one created by Kazuto Matsusaka, the chef-owner of the restaurant Zen Zero in Santa Monica. Kazuto warms the vinaigrette to serve with sautéed Arctic char, a fish related to salmon and trout that has deep orange-colored flesh, a delicate, moist texture, and a fine flake. I make the vinaigrette for steamed salmon but I haven't found a fish I don't like it with. (Arctic char also steams beautifully; if you can find it, steam two one-inch-thick fillets for five minutes.)

Chinese or garlic chives are a flat-leaved, garlic-scented member of the chive family used in Asian cooking; if you can find Chinese chives, they add a subtle note of garlic to the vinaigrette. If not, use regular chives or finely chopped scallion greens. Kazuto peels the tomatoes before chopping; this gives the tomato a softer, silkier texture, but it's an extra step that I don't always bother with.

The recipe makes enough vinaigrette to serve two generously with leftovers. The vinaigrette will keep for up to two days in the refrigerator; you can also use it to dress steamed green beans or broccoli.

TOMATO-SHALLOT VINAIGRETTE

1 medium to large ripe tomato (8 ounces)
$^1/_2$ teaspoon Dijon mustard
2 tablespoons balsamic vinegar
$^1/_2$ teaspoon salt
$^1/_4$ cup olive oil
$^1/_4$ cup finely chopped shallots (2 to 3 shallots)
2 tablespoons finely chopped Chinese (garlic) chives, or regular chives, or scallion greens
$^1/_8$ teaspoon freshly ground black pepper

2 salmon fillets (6 to 8 ounces each), about $1^1/_4$ inches thick at the thickest point
Salt

For the vinaigrette, first peel the tomato, if desired: Preheat the steamer. Cut a small X in the skin at the bottom of the tomato, opposite the stem end. Put the tomato in the steaming basket, cover, and steam until the skin loosens, about 2 minutes. Leaving the tomato in the basket, refresh under cold running water. Pull off the skin.

Core the tomato and cut it crosswise in half. Scoop out the seeds and juice with your fingers, and cut the tomato into small dice.

Put the mustard, vinegar, and salt in a medium jar with a lid or in a bowl. Shake or whisk together. Add the olive oil and shake to emulsify, or whisk in the oil in a thin stream, slowly at first until emulsified, and then more quickly. Add the tomato, shallots, chives or scallion greens, and pepper, and shake or whisk to blend. Taste and adjust the seasoning.

Place the salmon fillets, skin side down, in a single layer in the steaming basket, sprinkle with salt, cover, and steam until just barely cooked through but still translucent in the very center, 18 to 20 minutes. Set the steaming basket on a plate or in the sink and let the salmon stand, covered, while you warm the sauce.

Put the sauce in a medium saucepan and heat over medium heat, stirring occasionally, until it just comes to a simmer.

To serve, use a spatula to transfer the salmon to individual plates, and spoon the sauce on top.

Salmon with Quick Basil Oil

Serves 2

Water Level: Medium (Low if using the Waring)

Typically, recipes for basil-flavored oil blanch the basil to set the color and then combine it with oil to infuse for one or more days, enough time to let the basil give up its flavor to the oil. (Some puree the basil with the oil, some don't.) In this quick version, the basil is steamed rather than blanched and then steeped in warmed oil so the oil picks up the basil flavor within thirty minutes. I particularly like this oil on hot or cold salmon, but you can drizzle it over any steamed fish or chicken or vegetables. The oil will keep for a few weeks in the refrigerator.

continued

BASIL OIL
1 bunch basil (1 cup lightly packed leaves)
$^1\!/_2$ cup tasty olive oil
One 3- by 1-inch strip lemon zest

2 salmon fillets (6 to 8 ounces each), about 1$^1\!/_4$ inches thick at the thickest point
Salt and freshly ground black pepper

Pick the basil leaves off the stems, reserving stems for steaming the salmon. Place the leaves in the steaming basket, cover, and steam until the basil turns green, 30 to 45 seconds. Leaving the basil in the basket, refresh under cold running water. Squeeze out the excess water and coarsely chop.

Put the basil and oil in a small saucepan and heat over medium heat until just warm. Remove from the heat and let stand for 10 minutes. Add the lemon zest and let stand for 20 minutes longer.

Place the reserved basil stems in the steaming basket. Place the salmon, skin side down, in a single layer on the basil stems and sprinkle with salt. Cover and steam until the salmon is just barely cooked through but still translucent in the center, 18 to 20 minutes. Set the basket on a plate or in the sink and let the fish stand, covered, while you finish the oil.

Strain the oil through a fine strainer into a bowl, pressing on the basil to squeeze out as much oil as possible.

To serve, use a spatula to transfer the salmon to individual plates. Drizzle the oil over the fish and grind pepper over. Serve hot.

Red Snapper with Fresh Mango Chutney

Serves 2
Water Level: Medium (Low if using the Waring)

Red snapper is an exceptional fish: The white meat is firm and the flavor is distinctive without being strong. Even small snapper fillets are too large to fit in a single layer in electric steamers, but two fillets steam perfectly stacked on top of each other.

Use a ripe, sweet mango for the chutney, which is also particularly good with steamed shrimp, scallops, and lobster.

Fresh ginger is considerably more pungent when grated than when minced. I have a ceramic grater, made specially for grating ginger, but I like using the fine grating holes on a standard metal grater; the soft, edible part of the root passes through the holes and the tough fibers stay on the outside of the grater.

FRESH MANGO CHUTNEY

1 ripe mango
2 tablespoons chopped red onion
Grated zest and juice of 1 lime
$\frac{1}{2}$ jalapeño pepper, seeded, ribs removed, and finely minced
   (some seeds left in if you prefer the sauce spicy)
1 teaspoon chopped fresh coriander
$\frac{1}{4}$ teaspoon grated fresh ginger

2 red snapper fillets (about 6 ounces each), about $\frac{1}{2}$ inch thick at the
   thickest point
Salt

Aluminum foil

continued

For the chutney, stand the mango stem end up on a cutting board and cut down both flat sides with a large sharp knife to remove the fruit from the central seed in two large pieces. Discard the seed. Lay one piece of mango skin side down on the board and score the fruit into ½-inch dice, without cutting through the skin. Then, holding the knife almost parallel to the cutting board, slice the fruit off the skin. Repeat with the other piece of mango, and put the dice into a medium bowl. Add the remaining chutney ingredients and gently fold together without mashing the mango.

Cut a piece of aluminum foil slightly larger than a snapper fillet. Sprinkle both fillets lightly with salt and lay one, skin side down, on the foil. Lay the second fillet, skin up, on the first. Pick up the foil by opposite corners and set it in the steaming basket. Cover and steam until the fish is cooked through, 17 to 20 minutes. Set the basket on a plate or in the sink and let stand, covered, for about 2 minutes, to drain and finish cooling. Then pick up the foil again by opposite corners and put it on a cutting board. Cut the stacked fish in half crosswise and use a spatula to transfer the stacked fillets to individual plates. Spoon the chutney over the fish and serve.

Red Snapper with Rosemary Oil

Serves 2
Water Level: Medium (Low if using the Waring)

Rosemary and snapper partner each other surprisingly well; snapper has far and away enough flavor to stand up to the herb. Herb-infused oils are easy to put together and, because you need use very little of the strong-flavored oil, make a low-fat sauce for steamed fish, poultry, and vegetables. This oil needs to stand for forty-eight hours before it's ready to use. You'll need only a drizzle or two to flavor the snapper, but the leftover oil will keep for weeks.

ROSEMARY OIL

$\frac{1}{2}$ cup olive oil
$\frac{1}{4}$ cup chopped fresh rosemary
2 red snapper fillets (about 6 ounces each), about $\frac{1}{2}$ inch thick at the
   thickest point
Salt and freshly ground black pepper

Aluminum foil

For the oil, combine the oil and rosemary in a small jar. Put the lid on and refrigerate for 2 days. Then strain through a fine strainer and refrigerate until ready to use.

Cut a piece of aluminum foil slightly larger than a snapper fillet. Sprinkle both fillets lightly with salt and lay one, skin side down, on the foil. Lay the second fillet, skin up, on the first. Pick up the foil by opposite corners and set it in the steaming basket. Cover and steam until the fish is cooked through, 17 to 20 minutes. Set the basket on a plate or in the sink and let the fish stand, covered, for about 2 minutes, to drain and finish cooling. Then pick up the foil again by opposite corners and put it on a cutting board. Cut the stacked fish in half crosswise and use a spatula to transfer the stacked fillets to individual plates. Drizzle a tiny amount of the oil over the snapper, grind pepper over, and serve.

Red Snapper with Lemon and Ginger

Serves 2

Water Level: Medium (Low if using the Waring)

This lemon-ginger sauce is adapted from a recipe by Madhur Jaffrey. It's not really a sauce in the traditional sense, as, both hot and tart from the fresh ginger and lemon, it's very potent; I use it as a condiment— a little goes a long way.

2 red snapper fillets (about 6 ounces each), about $\frac{1}{2}$ inch thick at the thickest point

Aluminum foil

LEMON-GINGER SAUCE

1 tablespoon plus 1 teaspoon fresh lemon juice
2 tablespoons olive oil
1 teaspoon grated fresh ginger (see headnote, page 61)
1 tablespoon chopped fresh coriander

Cut a piece of aluminum foil slightly larger than a snapper fillet. Sprinkle both fillets lightly with salt and lay one, skin side down, on the foil. Lay the second fillet, skin up, on the first. Pick up the foil by opposite corners and set it in the steaming basket. Cover and steam until the fish is cooked through, 17 to 20 minutes. Set the basket on a plate or in the sink and let the fish stand, covered, about 2 minutes, to drain and finish cooking.

Meanwhile, stir together the sauce ingredients in a small bowl.

Pick up the foil again by opposite corners and put it on a cutting board. Cut the stacked fish in half crosswise and use a spatula to transfer the stacked fillets to individual plates. Drizzle the sauce over the fish and serve.

Halibut with Ginger, Scallion, and Toasted Sesame Seeds

Serves 2

Water Level: Medium (Low if using the Waring)

Halibut is a lean white fish, sold in either steaks or fillets; where I live in New York, I always see it as steaks. The steaks have a single central bone that is easy to remove, and no annoying little bones. Halibut steams beautifully, particularly in the rice bowl in a little liquid. (It will stick to the bowl, so oil it lightly.)

This recipe is inspired by one by Barbara Tropp for steamed lobster. You can make the recipe with fillets as well; steam them a few minutes less than the steaks. Serve the halibut with rice.

1 pound halibut steaks, 1$\frac{1}{4}$ to 1$\frac{1}{2}$ inches thick at the thickest point
1$\frac{1}{2}$ tablespoons soy sauce
1$\frac{1}{2}$ tablespoons rice wine vinegar
1$\frac{1}{2}$ teaspoons dark sesame oil
1 scallion, thinly sliced
$\frac{1}{2}$ teaspoon grated fresh ginger (see headnote, page 61)
1 teaspoon toasted sesame seeds

Aluminum foil

Brush or smear a little sesame oil over the bottom of the rice bowl, and place the halibut in a single layer in the bowl (see Equipment Notes).

Stir together the soy sauce, vinegar, sesame oil, scallion, and ginger and pour over the fish. Cover the rice bowl with aluminum foil, place in the steaming basket, cover, and steam until the halibut is cooked through but still translucent at the bone, 20 to 25 minutes. Use a spatula to transfer the fish to individual plates and spoon the juices over. Sprinkle with the sesame seeds and serve.

continued

• **Equipment Notes:** If using the Rival or Waring steamers, put the rice bowl directly on the steamer base, as described in the instruction manuals, rather than in the steaming basket.

Cod with Bell Peppers and Tomato

Serves 2

Water Level: Medium (Low if using the Waring)

If possible, use Turkish bay leaves in this recipe rather than the longer, narrower domestic leaves that are very strong-tasting, almost resinous. I like to steam cod steaks rather than fillets because fillets flake apart easily and so are hard to handle; steaks also stay moister.

Try this sauce with salmon, swordfish, tuna, shrimp, and chicken as well. Serve with steamed potatoes, rice, or bread to sop up the sauce.

<u>BASQUAISE SAUCE</u>

3 medium plum tomatoes, cored, or 1$\frac{1}{2}$ cups chopped canned Italian
   plum tomatoes with their juices
1 tablespoon olive oil
$\frac{1}{2}$ cup diced onions
$\frac{1}{2}$ red bell pepper, halved, cored, seeded, ribs removed, and cut
   lengthwise into $\frac{1}{4}$-inch-wide strips
$\frac{1}{2}$ green bell pepper, halved, cored, seeded, ribs removed, and cut
   lengthwise into $\frac{1}{4}$-inch-wide strips
1 garlic clove, minced
$\frac{1}{4}$ teaspoon salt, or more to taste
1 teaspoon balsamic vinegar or red wine vinegar
$\frac{1}{8}$ teaspoon freshly ground black pepper

4 large bay leaves (see headnote)
2 cod steaks (8 to 10 ounces each), $\frac{3}{4}$ to 1 inch thick
Salt and freshly ground black pepper

For the sauce, if using fresh tomatoes, preheat the steamer. Cut a small X in the skin at the bottom of the tomatoes, opposite the stem end. Put the tomatoes in the steaming basket, cover, and steam until the skin loosens, about 2 minutes. Leaving the tomatoes in the basket, refresh under cold running water. Pull off the skins. Core the tomatoes and cut them crosswise in half. Scoop out the seeds and juice with your fingers, and coarsely chop the tomatoes.

Heat the oil in a medium saucepan over medium heat. Add the onions, bell peppers, and salt and stir well. Cover and cook over medium-low heat, without browning, until the onions are translucent, about 5 minutes. Add the garlic and cook for 1 minute.

Add the chopped tomatoes, raise the heat, and simmer, uncovered, for 15 minutes. Add the vinegar and cook for 3 minutes; then add the pepper and taste for salt.

Meanwhile, put 2 bay leaves in either side of the steaming basket. Sprinkle the cod on both sides with salt and put the cod steaks on top of the leaves. Cover and steam until the cod is just cooked through but still translucent at the bone, about 15 minutes. Set the steaming basket on a plate or in the sink and let the fish stand, covered, for about 2 minutes to finish cooking and drain.

To serve, spoon the sauce onto plates, place the cod on top, discarding the bay leaves, and grind pepper over.

Two Green Sauces for Cod

I love fresh herb vinaigrettes made in the style of the traditional Italian *salsa verde*, or green sauce. They're thick with herbs, chopped capers and, sometimes, anchovy, and tart with lemon. Here are two such vinaigrettes, particularly good with cod, but suitable for almost any fish, particularly steamed snapper, salmon, and swordfish; both serve two generously. Serve the fish with bread or boiled or steamed potatoes to soak up the sauce. The sherry vinaigrette is adapted from a favorite of mine in Jacques Manière's *Cuisine à la Vapeur.*

Parsley-Lemon Vinaigrette

1/4 cup chopped flat-leaf parsley
2 tablespoons olive oil
1 tablespoon drained small capers, finely chopped
2 teaspoons fresh lemon juice
1/4 teaspoon salt
1/8 teaspoon freshly ground black pepper

In a small bowl, whisk together all of the ingredients. (The vinaigrette can be made several hours in advance, but don't add the lemon juice until just before serving.)

Sherry Vinaigrette

1 tablespoon chopped flat-leaf parsley
2 teaspoons chopped fresh chives or scallion green
1 tablespoon drained small capers, finely chopped
2 teaspoons sherry vinegar
1 anchovy fillet, finely chopped (optional)
1/8 teaspoon salt
1/8 teaspoon freshly ground black pepper
2 tablespoons olive oil

In a small bowl, whisk together all the ingredients.

Fresh Tuna Salade Niçoise

Serves 4

Water Level: High (see Equipment Notes)

Traditionally, this salad from France's Mediterranean coast is made with canned tuna, but fresh tuna is prettier and transforms the salad into something of a luxury. The vegetables are usually blanched (some versions call for roasted peppers), but steaming is easier and faster.

The tuna and vegetables can be steamed several hours ahead and then refrigerated to marinate in the vinaigrette. Slice the tomatoes and peel and quarter the eggs just before serving.

If you like, make the salad with swordfish steaks, salmon fillets, or boneless, skinless chicken breasts.

BALSAMIC VINAIGRETTE

1/4 cup plus 2 tablespoons balsamic vinegar
1 tablespoon plus 1 teaspoon Dijon mustard
1/4 teaspoon salt
1/8 teaspoon freshly ground black pepper
1/4 cup plus 2 tablespoons olive oil

2 large eggs
1 tablespoon coarsely chopped fresh basil, stems reserved
1 pound tuna steak, 3/4 to 1 inch thick
Salt
1 pound medium red or white waxy potatoes, quartered but not peeled
1/2 pound green beans, trimmed
1 red bell pepper, halved, cored, seeded, and ribs removed
1 green bell pepper, halved, cored, seeded, and ribs removed
Freshly ground black pepper
3/4 teaspoon chopped fresh thyme or 1/4 teaspoon dried
1/4 cup Niçoise olives, drained
1 small head Boston lettuce, washed and dried
1 large ripe tomato, cored and cut into 8 wedges
One 6-ounce jar marinated artichoke hearts (preferably Cara Mia),
    drained

continued

For the vinaigrette, put the vinegar, mustard, salt, and pepper in a small jar and shake to combine. Or whisk together in a small bowl. Add the oil to the jar and shake to emulsify, or whisk in the oil. Set aside.

Place the eggs in one side of the steaming basket, cover, and steam for 7 minutes. Open the steamer and place the basil stems in the other side of the basket. Sprinkle the tuna on both sides with salt and place on top of the basil stems. Cover and steam until the tuna is medium-rare, about 15 minutes. Transfer the eggs to a bowl of cold water, and transfer the tuna to a plate.

Put the potatoes in a single layer in the steaming basket, cover, and steam for 10 minutes. Push the potatoes to one side, add the beans and bell peppers, and steam until all the vegetables are tender, about 20 minutes longer.

Meanwhile, cut the tuna into 1/4-inch-thick strips and place in a bowl. Grind pepper over the tuna, pour about one third of the vinaigrette over, add the chopped basil, and toss carefully to coat the tuna. Set aside.

When the vegetables are cooked, transfer the potatoes to a bowl. Leaving the beans and peppers in the steaming basket, refresh them under cold running water. Drain well and pat dry on paper towels.

Pour half of the remaining vinaigrette over the potatoes, add the thyme, and toss to coat.

Cut the peppers into 1/2-inch-wide strips. Put the peppers and beans in another bowl, add the remaining vinaigrette, and toss to coat.

Peel the eggs and cut lengthwise into quarters. Place the olives in a single layer on a cutting board and smash them with the bottom of a saucepan; pull out the pits.

To serve, line a serving plate with the lettuce leaves. Mound the tuna in the center of the plate and arrange the potatoes, peppers, and beans in piles around it. Put the tomato wedges in the bowl that held the beans and peppers and the artichoke hearts in the potato bowl. Toss with the vinaigrette remaining in the bowls, and arrange on the salad plate. Place the eggs, yolks up, on the plate, sprinkle the olives over all, and pour any remaining vinaigrette over the lettuce leaves.

• **Equipment Notes:** If using the Waring, fill the reservoir to Low to steam the eggs and tuna. Then add more boiling water to steam the vegetables.

Tuna with Tapenade

Serves 2

Water Level: Medium (Low if using the Waring)

Some cooks prefer to make tapenade with the shiny, slightly shriveled, Greek oil-cured olives, while others swear by the little Niçoise olives in brine. Although not particularly traditional, grated orange zest adds a floral counterpoint to the rich, salty tapenade; add some if you like. This recipe makes more than enough tapenade for two; it holds several days in the refrigerator.

TAPENADE

1 cup black olives, such as Niçoise or Gaeta, pitted (see page 70)
1 garlic clove, coarsely chopped
2 anchovy fillets (optional)
1 tablespoon drained small capers
1/2 teaspoon fresh thyme leaves or 1/4 teaspoon dried
Pinch of cayenne pepper
3 tablespoons olive oil

2 tuna steaks (6 to 8 ounces each), 3/4 to 1 inch thick
Salt and freshly ground black pepper
2 teaspoons coarsely chopped flat-leaf parsley

Combine the tapenade ingredients in a food processor and process to a paste. Scrape into a small serving bowl.

Sprinkle the tuna on both sides with salt and put it in a single layer in the steaming basket. Steam until medium-rare, about 15 minutes. Set the basket on a plate or in the sink and let the fish stand, covered, for about 2 minutes, to drain and finish cooking. Put each tuna steak on an individual plate. Grind pepper over and sprinkle with the parsley. Serve the tapenade on the side.

Swordfish with Lemon-Caper Vinaigrette

Serves 2

Water Level: Medium (Low if using the Waring)

We're used to eating swordfish grilled or sautéed, so steaming it may seem odd. In fact, however, steamed swordfish is superb—moist, tender, and meaty—and some traditional Italian recipes do call for steaming it. I steam the fish until it's just rare in the center, but it finishes cooking as it stands. This vinaigrette tastes good on almost any fish; try it on salmon, tuna, cod, or snapper.

LEMON-CAPER VINAIGRETTE

1 tablespoon fresh lemon juice
2 tablespoons olive oil
1 teaspoon drained small capers, chopped
8 Niçoise olives, drained, pitted (see page 70), and coarsely chopped
$1/8$ teaspoon salt, or more to taste
Pinch of freshly ground black pepper, or more to taste

2 swordfish steaks (6 to 8 ounces each), about 1 inch thick
Salt and freshly ground black pepper

For the vinaigrette, put all the ingredients in a jar, cover, and shake to emulsify. Or whisk together in a bowl. Taste for seasoning.

Sprinkle the steaks on both sides with salt and put them in a single layer in the steaming basket. Cover and steam until the fish is rare in the center, 12 to 14 minutes. Set the steaming basket on a plate or in the sink and let the fish stand, covered, for about 2 minutes, to drain and finish cooking.

Place the fish on individual plates and grind pepper over. Spoon the sauce over the fish and serve.

Swordfish with Red Pepper Butter

Serves 2

Water Level: Medium (Low if using the Waring)

The compound butter in this recipe is flavored with steamed red bell pepper. Steaming accentuates both the sweet taste and underlying bite of the pepper. It's easy to make; if the butter is softened to room temperature, the whole thing can be done in the blender. I like this butter on cod and tuna too, as well as on chicken. The fish or chicken must be hot so the butter melts over it. Half a teaspoon of Tabasco may seem like a lot of hot sauce, but the butter is only mildly spicy.

The recipe makes extra pepper butter—enough to serve eight to ten—but it will keep for a few days in the refrigerator or several weeks in the freezer; just cut off quarter-inch-thick medallions from the log of chilled butter for each serving of hot fish.

RED PEPPER BUTTER

$^1/_2$ red bell pepper, cored, seeded, and ribs removed
1 large garlic clove, chopped
$^1/_2$ teaspoon red wine vinegar
$^1/_2$ teaspoon Tabasco sauce
$^1/_2$ teaspoon salt
8 tablespoons (1 stick) butter, at room temperature

2 swordfish steaks (6 to 8 ounces each), about $1^1/_4$ inches thick
Salt

Parchment paper or aluminum foil

For the butter, place the bell pepper in the steaming basket, cover, and steam for 15 minutes. Leaving the pepper in the steaming basket, refresh under cold running water. Drain well and pat dry.

Transfer the pepper to a blender and add the garlic, vinegar, Tabasco, and salt. Blend to puree. Add the butter and blend until smooth. (The finished butter will be very loose.) Set aside.

continued

Sprinkle the fish on both sides with salt and put it in a single layer in the steaming basket. Cover and steam until the fish is almost cooked through but still rare at the center, 12 to 14 minutes. Set the steaming basket on a plate or in the sink and let stand, covered, for 2 minutes, to drain and finish cooking.

Use a spatula to transfer the fish to individual plates. Spoon about 1 tablespoonful of the butter onto each piece of fish and serve immediately. Roll the remaining butter into a log in parchment paper or foil and refrigerate or freeze.

Swordfish with Anchovy Mayonnaise

Serves 2
Water Level: Medium (Low if using the Waring)

Swordfish is lean, particularly when steamed, and therefore benefits from a luxurious mayonnaise like this one, softly flavored with anchovy but with a surprise kick of spice.

2 swordfish steaks (6 to 8 ounces each), about 1 inch thick
Salt and freshly ground black pepper
Anchovy Mayonnaise (page 23), made with 2 tablespoons lemon juice

Sprinkle the fish steaks on both sides with salt and put them in a single layer in the steaming basket. Cover and steam until the fish is rare in the center, 12 to 14 minutes. Set the steaming basket on a plate or in the sink and let the fish stand, covered, for 2 minutes to drain and cook through completely.

Place the fish on individual plates and grind pepper over. Spoon a generous dollop of the mayonnaise on each, and serve.

Monkfish with Black Pepper–Mustard Sauce

Serves 2
Water Level: Medium (Low if using the Waring)

Monkfish is a particularly firm white-fleshed fish—its texture is often compared to lobster. Although ten years ago it was hard to find monkfish in American fish stores, it's more available now. The boneless fillets are covered with a purplish-gray membrane; ask your fish store to trim it, or trim it yourself until you can see the pure white meat underneath. Like lobster, monkfish needs to be cooked completely, or it's chewy; it cooks perfectly in the steamer without drying out. Don't be scared away by the cream in this recipe; it's a very little bit and thinned with the monkfish steaming liquid. Monkfish is lean and needs this richness.

I make this recipe with two small fillets but it will work just as well with one larger fillet. Just increase the steaming time by about five minutes. Serve with boiled or steamed potatoes.

BLACK PEPPER–MUSTARD SAUCE

¼ **cup light cream**
2 **tablespoons Dijon mustard**
¼ **teaspoon cracked black pepper**

1 **pound trimmed monkfish fillet, about 1 inch thick at the thickest point**
Salt

For the sauce, whisk together the cream and mustard in a medium saucepan (off the heat). Add the pepper and set aside.

Sprinkle the fish on both sides with salt and put it in a single layer in the steaming basket. Cover and steam until cooked through, about 15 minutes. Set the basket on a plate or in the sink and let the fish stand, covered, to keep warm while you finish the sauce.

continued

Spoon out 2 tablespoons of the steaming liquid from the drip pan, or the water reservoir if using the Waring, and whisk into the sauce (see Equipment Notes). Bring the sauce just to a boil.

Use a spatula to transfer the fish to individual plates. Spoon the sauce over each fillet and serve.

• **Equipment Notes:** If using the Rival, use a bulb baster to retrieve the steaming liquid.

Shrimp with Black Beans and Mango

Serves 2

Water Level: Medium (Low if using the Waring)

To make this main-course salad even easier, replace the tomato, onion, and jalapeño pepper with half a cup of strained store-bought salsa. If you're using a fresh jalapeño, remember that they vary in spiciness and that most of the heat is in the seeds and ribs. Leave in the seeds and ribs if you like hot food.

Although most supermarkets and fish stores sell shrimp graded as jumbo, large, medium, or small, these terms aren't regulated and don't mean much. The best way to choose shrimp is the way it is sold in the industry, where it is graded by number of shrimp to the pound. (Ask the counterperson, or simply count how many shrimp are in a one-pound package.) As a general rule, the smaller the shrimp, the cheaper it is; smaller, less expensive shrimp are perfect for this salad.

Some canned black beans are broken and mushy; Goya beans are firm and whole and very good in this salad.

1 pound small (26 to 35 count) shrimp, peeled and deveined
One 16-ounce can black beans, rinsed and drained
1 medium tomato, cored and chopped
$1/4$ cup chopped red onion
$1/2$ jalapeño pepper (or to taste), seeded, ribs removed, and minced
    (some seeds and ribs left in if you like spicy food)
1 tablespoon chopped fresh coriander, plus 8 to 10 leaves for garnish
Juice of 1 lime
1 tablespoon olive oil
$1/4$ teaspoon salt, or more to taste
4 good-quality flour tortillas
1 ripe mango
6 to 8 leaves Boston lettuce, washed and dried

Arrange the shrimp in a single layer in the steaming basket, cover, and steam until just cooked through, 8 to 10 minutes. Remove from the steamer and let cool.

Put the beans, tomato, onion, jalapeño, coriander, lime juice, olive oil, and salt in a medium bowl and toss to mix. Add the cooled shrimp and toss gently. Taste for seasoning.

Wrap the tortillas in aluminum foil and warm in a preheated 325°F oven for 6 to 8 minutes.

Meanwhile, set the mango stem end up on a cutting board and cut down both flat sides with a large sharp knife to remove the fruit from the flat central seed in two large pieces. Discard the seed. Lay one piece of the mango skin side down on the board and score the fruit into $1/2$-inch dice, without cutting through the skin. Then, holding the knife almost parallel to the cutting board, slice the fruit off the skin. Repeat with the other piece of mango.

To serve, line a shallow serving bowl or plate with the lettuce leaves. Mound the shrimp salad on the lettuce and scatter the mango over the top. Garnish with coriander leaves, and serve with warm tortillas.

Maryland Spiced Shrimp

Serves 2 generously

Water Level: Medium (Low if using the Waring)

These shrimp are great snack or party food. They're fast and easy and can be made several hours ahead. The fun of them is in the peeling and finger licking. This recipe serves two generously but can be increased to serve any number of guests. If necessary, steam the shrimp in batches: It must be steamed in a single layer, or it won't cook evenly. Serve with ice-cold beer.

1 pound small shrimp (26 to 35 count), in the shell
1 generous tablespoon Old Bay Seasoning

Put the shrimp in a single layer in the steaming basket, cover, and steam until the shrimp turns pink, 8 to 10 minutes (you may need to cook it in two batches). Dump the shrimp into a bowl, add the Old Bay Seasoning, and stir or toss to coat the shrimp with the seasoning. Cover and refrigerate until well chilled, about 2 hours.

Shrimp with White Beans and Rosemary

Serves 2

Water Level: Medium (Low if using the Waring)

The beans in this dish should be very juicy; if the tomato mixture gets too dry, add a little water. If you have the time, dried beans that you soak and cook yourself are tastier and firmer than canned. The second tablespoon of olive oil added at the end of the recipe sauces the beans divinely, but you can get away without it if you're concerned about fat.

1 tablespoon butter
2 tablespoons tasty olive oil
$\frac{1}{4}$ cup chopped onion
$\frac{1}{4}$ cup chopped celery
1 small garlic clove, minced
$\frac{1}{2}$ teaspoon chopped fresh rosemary or $\frac{1}{4}$ teaspoon dried
1 cup chopped ripe tomatoes or canned Italian plum tomatoes
1 tablespoon chopped flat-leaf parsley
2 tablespoons dry white wine plus 2 tablespoons water or $\frac{1}{4}$ cup water
$\frac{1}{2}$ teaspoon salt
$\frac{1}{8}$ teaspoon freshly ground black pepper
2 cups cooked white (cannellini) beans (one 19-ounce can)
1 pound medium (16 to 25 count) shrimp, peeled and deveined,
**   tails left on**

Melt the butter with 1 tablespoon of the oil in a medium saucepan over medium-low heat. Add the onion, celery, garlic, and rosemary, cover, and cook, without browning, until the onion is translucent, about 5 minutes. Stir in the tomatoes, parsley, water or water and wine, salt, and pepper. Bring to a simmer, cover, and simmer gently for 5 minutes. Remove from the heat and set aside.

Meanwhile, if using canned beans, drain, rinse under cold running water, and drain again.

Put the shrimp in a single layer in the steaming basket, cover, and steam until pink and just cooked through, about 12 minutes. Set the steaming basket on a plate or in the sink and let stand, covered, to drain.

Pour the steaming liquid from the drip pan, or about ⅓ cup of the water from the reservoir if using the Waring, into the tomato mixture (see Equipment Notes). Bring to a simmer, add the beans, and cook for 1 to 2 minutes, to heat through. Remove from the heat, add the shrimp and the remaining 1 tablespoon olive oil, and stir gently. Serve immediately.

• **Equipment Notes:** If using the Rival, use a bulb baster to retrieve the steaming liquid for the sauce.

Scallops Marco Polo

Serves 2
Water Level: Medium (Low if using the Waring)
Preheat the Steamer

The name of this recipe is a play on the fact that the sauce combines both Asian and Italian ingredients. Steaming uncovers the delicate sweetness of fresh scallops and keeps them moist and velvety tender. Don't overcook them or they will toughen. Serve with white rice.

¾ **pound medium asparagus, stalks trimmed and cut on the diagonal into 3 pieces each**
¾ **to 1 pound sea scallops, tough side muscles removed**
Salt

MARCO POLO SAUCE

1 teaspoon olive oil

1 scallion, chopped

1 teaspoon chopped garlic

1 teaspoon grated fresh ginger (see headnote, page 61)

1/8 teaspoon hot red pepper flakes (optional)

1 tablespoon soy sauce

1 tablespoon dry sherry

1 tablespoon balsamic vinegar

1 tablespoon sugar

1/4 cup chicken stock or canned low-sodium broth

1 1/2 tablespoons cornstarch, dissolved in 1 tablespoon cold chicken stock
    or canned low-sodium broth

8 small fresh basil leaves, cut into thin slivers

Preheat the steamer. Put the asparagus in the steaming basket, cover, and steam until just tender, 6 to 8 minutes; toss halfway through the steaming time to bring the asparagus on the bottom up to the top. Leaving the asparagus in the steaming basket, refresh under cold running water. Drain and transfer to a plate.

Sprinkle the scallops with salt and put them in a single layer in the steaming basket. Cover and steam until just firm to the touch, 8 to 10 minutes for medium scallops, 12 to 15 minutes for large.

Meanwhile, heat the oil in a large nonstick pan over medium-high heat. Add the scallion, garlic, ginger, and the red pepper flakes, if using, and cook, stirring, until fragrant, about 30 seconds. Stir in the asparagus, then stir in the soy sauce, sherry, vinegar, sugar, and stock or broth and bring to a boil. Stir the cornstarch mixture to remix, stir it into the sauce, and bring just to a boil, stirring until the sauce thickens. Remove from the heat and cover to keep warm.

When the scallops are cooked, set the steaming basket on a plate or in the sink and let stand, covered, for 2 minutes to drain.

Divide the scallops between two plates. Pour the sauce over, sprinkle with the basil, and serve.

Scallops with Lime Butter

Serves 2

Water Level: Medium (Low if using the Waring)

Very easy and very delicious.

¾ to 1 pound sea scallops, tough side muscles removed
Salt
Grated zest of 1 lime
1 tablespoon fresh lime juice
2 tablespoons chilled butter, cut into bits
Pinch of freshly ground black pepper

Sprinkle the scallops with salt and put them in a single layer in the steaming basket. Cover and steam until firm to the touch, 8 to 10 minutes for medium scallops, 12 to 15 minutes for large ones. Set the basket on a plate or in the sink and let stand, covered, to drain while you make the sauce.

Pour the juices from the drip pan into a medium frying pan (see Equipment Notes), add the zest, and bring to a boil over high heat. Boil until reduced to 1 to 2 tablespoons. Add the lime juice and bring to a boil. Whisk in the butter bit by bit until emulsfied. Whisk in a pinch of salt and the pepper, and remove from the heat.

Put the scallops on individual plates, pour the sauce over, and serve.

• **Equipment Notes:** If using the Rival, use a bulb baster to retrieve the steaming liquid. If using the Waring, reduce the liquid from the reservoir just as you would the juices from the drip pan; use a large frying pan to speed the reduction.

Steamed Clams with Butter and Lemon

Serves 2

Water Level: Medium (Low if using the Waring)

In Maine, clam lovers prefer to eat their steamed clams dipped in melted butter and then drink the juices separately. I suggest sixteen to twenty clams for two, but my experience is that the clams get devoured practically immediately regardless of how many there are. If you like spicy clams, add a couple of dashes of Tabasco to the butter. Serve this as a first course or an afternoon snack with a cold beer. Make sure there's a bowl on the table for the shells.

16 to 20 littleneck clams

LEMON BUTTER SAUCE

2 tablespoons butter, melted
1 teaspoon fresh lemon juice
2 to 3 dashes of Tabasco sauce (optional)

Clean the clams well by putting them in a bowl of cold water to cover and scrubbing the shells with a stiff brush. Change the water two or three times, and scrub the clams until there is no longer any sand at the bottom of the bowl when the water is changed.

Put the clams in the steaming basket, cover, and steam until they open, 15 to 20 minutes.

Meanwhile, combine the butter, lemon juice, and the Tabasco, if using, in a small bowl.

Transfer the clams to a serving bowl, discarding any that have not opened. Pour the juices from the drip tray into glasses, if you like, to drink. Serve the clams with the lemon butter.

Spaghetti with Clams

Serves 2

Water Level: Medium (Low if using the Waring)

I developed this recipe as a low-fat version of spaghetti with white clam sauce. The sauce is simply the juices from the clams that collect in the drip pan or reservoir during steaming, flavored with shallot, garlic, and a couple of teaspoons of olive oil. Because the sauce is made with little else than their juices, it tastes of pure clams.

The two teaspoons oil in the recipe are just enough to add flavor and a little richness to the sauce—but if you're not counting fat grams, it's even better with two to four tablespoons. Serve with spoons or bread to sop up the sauce.

18 littleneck clams
1 medium shallot, chopped
1 medium garlic clove, minced
Salt
$^1/_2$ pound spaghetti
1 tablespoon chopped flat-leaf parsley
2 teaspoons olive oil
**$^1/_4$ teaspoon hot red pepper flakes or pinch of freshly ground
    black pepper**

Clean the clams well by putting them in a bowl of cold water to cover and scrubbing the shells with a stiff brush. Change the water two or three times, and scrub the clams until there is no longer any sand at the bottom of the bowl when the water is changed.

Bring a large pot of water to a boil for the spaghetti.

Put the shallot and garlic in the drip pan, or in the reservoir if using the Waring. Put the clams in the steaming basket, cover, and steam until the clams open, 15 to 20 minutes if using the Black & Decker or the West Bend, 12 to 14 minutes if using the Rival or Waring (see Equipment Notes). Discard any clams that do not open.

Meanwhile, salt the boiling water (it should taste salty) and cook the spaghetti until al dente, about 12 minutes. Drain in a colander and transfer to a large pasta or shallow serving bowl.

Add the clams in their shells (or shelled, if you prefer) and the juices in the drip pan, or reduced liquid from the reservoir, along with the shallot and garlic. Add the parsley, oil, red pepper flakes or black pepper, toss, and serve.

• **Equipment Notes:** If using the Waring, remove the steaming basket from the base and boil the steaming liquid, uncovered, in the reservoir until reduced to about 1 cup, or the Low line.

VARIATION

Spaghetti with Red Clam Sauce

Steam the clams open as above, but omit the shallot and garlic. Start cooking the spaghetti when the clams are only 5 minutes away from opening. When the clams open, remove the steaming basket to a plate or the sink. Discard any clams that have not opened, and cover the basket to keep warm. Pour half the juices from the drip pan, or the reservoir if using the Waring, into a large frying pan. Add ½ cup Tomato Sauce (page 115), bring to a boil over high heat, and boil until thickened and reduced to between ¾ and 1 cup, about 5 minutes. Put the hot drained spaghetti in the serving bowl, add the sauce, clams, and parsley (omit the olive oil), and toss well. (If you like, shell the clams and rewarm them in the sauce just before tossing with the pasta.) Sprinkle with the red pepper flakes or black pepper.

Mussels Fra Diavolo

Serves 2
Water Level: Medium (Low if using the Waring)

Fra Diavolo is a spicy tomato sauce. Double the recipe to serve four if you like; two pounds mussels take about the same time to steam as one pound.

FRA DIAVOLO SAUCE

1 tablespoon olive oil
$^1/_2$ cup chopped onions
1 garlic clove, minced
1 cup canned Italian plum tomatoes, with their juices
1 tablespoon balsamic vinegar
1 tablespoon chopped flat-leaf parsley
$^1/_2$ teaspoon salt
$^1/_4$ teaspoon hot red pepper flakes

$^1/_2$ pound linguine
1 pound small mussels, preferably cultivated (20 to 25 mussels), scrubbed
   and debearded
Salt

Bring a large pot of water to a boil for the pasta.

For the sauce, heat the oil in a medium saucepan over medium heat. Add the onions and cook, stirring, without browning, until translucent, about 4 minutes. Add the garlic and cook for 1 minute. Add the tomatoes with their juices, the vinegar, parsley, salt, and red pepper flakes. Break up the tomatoes with a wooden spoon and stir to combine. Bring to a simmer, reduce the heat, and simmer, uncovered, for 10 minutes. Remove from the heat.

Start the mussels and the pasta cooking at the same time: Place the mussels in the steaming basket, cover, and steam until they open, about 15 minutes. Salt the boiling pasta water heavily, add the pasta, and cook just until al dente.

Drain the pasta and dump into a large shallow bowl. Return the pasta sauce to a simmer, and pour it over the pasta.

As soon as the mussels are cooked, add them to the pasta and toss. Serve immediately.

Lobster Tails with Sweet Red Pepper Mayonnaise

Serves 2

Water Level: High (Low if using the Waring)

Tails from spiny lobsters are sold frozen in many supermarkets and fish stores. Spiny lobsters, found in warm and cold waters around the world, don't have the large front claws of the North American lobster, and the flavor of the meat is a bit different. Frozen tails can be steamed without thawing; the flavor and texture is every bit as good as if they were thawed first.

You can make the red pepper mayonnaise with homemade mayo or with store-bought regular or low-fat mayonnaise. Serve the lobster tails warm, at room temperature, or cold.

RED PEPPER MAYONNAISE

$1/2$ **medium red bell pepper, cored, seeded, and ribs removed**
$1/4$ **cup mayonnaise, homemade (page 24) or store-bought**
1 garlic clove, coarsely chopped
$1/2$ **teaspoon red wine vinegar**
$1/8$ **teaspoon salt, or more to taste**
$1/8$ **teaspoon freshly ground black pepper, or more to taste**
Pinch of cayenne pepper

2 lobster tails (8 to 10 ounces each) thawed or still frozen   *continued*

For the mayonnaise, put the pepper in the steaming basket, cover, and steam until tender, about 15 minutes. Let cool for a few minutes, and then pull off the skin with your fingers.

Put the pepper in a food processor or blender and process to a puree. Add the remaining mayonnaise ingredients and process to mix. Let stand for about 15 minutes, then taste and adjust the seasoning (the cayenne needs about 15 minutes for the heat to bloom).

Put the lobster tails in a single layer in the steaming basket, cover, and steam until cooked through, about 17 minutes for thawed tails, 25 to 30 minutes for frozen. To test for doneness, remove one tail from the steamer and feel the underside—the meat should be firm; and gently pull apart the exposed meat at the wide end of the tail and peer inside—the meat should no longer be translucent.

When the tails are cooked, remove them from the steamer and wrap in a clean towel. Set them on their sides and press down sharply on each one with the palm of your hand to crack the shell. Remove from the towel and use kitchen scissors to cut open the underside of the shell. Pull the meat out. Slice the meat crosswise into half-inch-thick medallions and serve hot, at room temperature, or cold, with the mayonnaise.

• **Note:** You can also use the steamer to precook frozen lobster tails before broiling: Put them in the steamer frozen and steam them as described in the recipe above, but undercook them by a few minutes. Use kitchen scissors to cut open the rounded top side of the shells. Force the shells open and slit open the tails with a knife, cutting about halfway through the flesh. Stuff with butter and broil until lightly browned, 2 to 3 minutes.

Seafood Salad

Serves 2 as a main course or 4 as an appetizer
Water Level: Medium (Low if using the Waring)

This recipe is adapted from my memory of a salad Alfred Portale makes at the Gotham Bar and Grill in New York City, far and away the best seafood salad I've ever eaten. There's little else in the recipe but seafood, lemon juice, olive oil, and fresh herbs, so it's critical that all the ingredients be of excellent quality. Here's the place to use a really good olive oil; I like a spicy Tuscan oil. Lemon juice varies in acidity, so you need to taste as you go.

If you're in a hurry, the seafood can all be cooled immediately in the steaming basket under cold running water.

20 small (31 to 35 count) shrimp, peeled and deveined
10 ounces sea scallops, tough side muscles removed
Salt
12 mussels, preferably cultivated, scrubbed and debearded
$^1/_3$ pound cleaned squid, bodies cut crosswise into $^1/_8$- to $^1/_4$-inch rings and tentacle sections cut in half

LEMON VINAIGRETTE

Grated zest of 1 lemon
2 tablespoons fresh lemon juice, or more to taste
1 tablespoon chopped flat-leaf parsley
2 teaspoons chopped fresh chives
1 teaspoon chopped fresh tarragon
$^1/_4$ teaspoon salt, or more to taste
Pinch of freshly ground black pepper, or more to taste
2 tablespoons good tasting extra virgin olive oil

1 avocado, cut lengthwise in half, pitted, and peeled

Line a plate or baking dish large enough to hold all of the seafood with three layers of paper towels.

continued

Place the shrimp in a single layer in the steaming basket, cover, and steam until they turn pink, 8 to 10 minutes. Dump the shrimp out onto the towel-lined plate, cover, and refrigerate.

Put the scallops in a single layer in the steaming basket, sprinkle with salt, cover, and steam until they open, 3 to 5 minutes. Add them to the plate with the shrimp, cover, and refrigerate.

Put the mussels in a single layer in the steaming basket, cover, and steam them until they open, 3 to 5 minutes. Add to the other seafood, cover, and refrigerate.

Put the squid in the steaming basket, sprinkle with salt, cover, and steam until just cooked through, about 3 minutes (be careful not to overcook). Add to the rest of the seafood, cover, and refrigerate until cold, about 30 minutes.

Meanwhile, make the vinaigrette: In a bowl large enough to hold the seafood, whisk together the lemon zest and juice, herbs, salt, and pepper. Whisk in the olive oil. Taste for seasoning and lemon juice; the vinaigrette should be tart.

Shell the mussels and cut the scallops into thin rounds. Add all the seafood into the vinaigrette and toss.

If serving four, cut the avocado halves lengthwise in half again.

Lay a quarter or half of the avocado, pit side down, on a cutting board. Starting about 1 inch from the stem end, cut the avocado lengthwise into thin slices, leaving them connected at the stem end. Press down on the avocado gently with the palm of your hand to fan it, and place the fan on an individual serving plate. Repeat with the remaining avocado. Spoon the salad across the center of the avocado slices, so that the slices peek out, and serve.

Poultry and Meat

T hink the notion of steamed chicken and meat sounds weird? So did I before I starting on my steaming odyssey and became a total convert. But steaming is a terrific way to cook many cuts, particularly if you're looking for a way to cut down on fat. Those same lean cuts of chicken, turkey, duck, and beef that are recommended for healthy diets dry out easily during cooking because they haven't much fat; steaming keeps them moist. Once steamed, poultry skin pulls off easily to make even the dark meat especially lean. Fatty pork and lamb ribs can be steamed before roasting to get rid of much of their fat. A steamed lean steak is so juicy and meaty-tasting that you don't miss the marbling. Beef shin, an underrated cut of beef if there ever was one, is absolutely superb steamed.

The size of these steamers dictates the types of poultry and cuts of meat we can cook in them. As with fish, most meat, with the exception of ribs, which are cooked for a long time, must be cooked in a single layer to steam properly. Cornish game hens are therefore a perfect size for the machines, as are chicken breasts—both boneless and skinless and on the bone. Two boneless duck breasts or two legs fit easily into the baskets. Lean ground turkey and beef can be steamed as meat balls or loaves, and turkey cutlets make tidy balls when wrapped around a filling.

Poultry and meat render a substantial amount of very flavorful juices while they steam. This broth falls into the drip pan (or the reservoir if you're using the Waring), and it's a gold mine. Pour it into a container and refrigerate it. The fat rises to the top and solidifies so that it's easily scraped off with a spoon. The broth can be frozen, or it will keep for at least a week in the refrigerator; be sure to bring it to a boil every two to three days, as you would stock. (I usually refrigerate it with the fat left on top; the fat seems to lengthen the life of the broth.) Use the broth for making rice dishes, soups, and sauces.

Cornish game hens give off so much juice, and ribs so much fat, that you need to be careful when using the West Bend that the drip pan doesn't overflow. Check it at least once during steaming. For the same reason, the reservoir on the Waring should be filled only to the Low or Medium mark; any more water, and it will bubble up into the steaming basket and poach the hens or ribs.

As is true of other cooking methods, the juices flee to the center of poultry and meat as it steams. It's important, therefore, to let poultry and meat rest for about five minutes after steaming to allow the juices to be reabsorbed throughout the meat. It's easy to do this with the steamer; just set the basket, covered, on a plate. The food will stay warm as it rests.

Soy-Orange–Marinated Chicken Cutlets

Serves 4
Water Level: Medium

Just twenty minutes in a marinade before steaming adds a lot of flavor to low-in-fat boneless, skinless chicken breasts and keeps the meat moist. Use brined kosher-style breasts (such as Empire brand) if you can find them. Serve with rice and steamed broccoli.

This marinade/vinaigrette can be used with steak or fish as well.

SOY-ORANGE VINAIGRETTE

2 tablespoons fresh orange juice
1 tablespoon hoisin sauce
1 tablespoon soy sauce
2 teaspoons seasoned or plain rice wine vinegar
$^1/_2$ teaspoon dark sesame oil
1 scallion, chopped
1 tablespoon chopped fresh coriander
1 teaspoon grated fresh ginger (see headnote, page 61)
$^1/_8$ teaspoon freshly ground black pepper

4 boneless, skinless chicken breast halves (1 to 1$^1/_4$ pounds total)
1 teaspoon toasted sesame seeds

continued

For the vinaigrette, combine all of the ingredients in a shallow bowl large enough to hold the chicken. Add the chicken and turn to coat. Cover and refrigerate for at least 20 minutes, or up to 2 hours.

Remove the chicken from the bowl, reserving the vinaigrette, and put it in a single layer in the steaming basket. Cover and steam until the chicken is cooked through and the juices run clear when the thickest part is pierced with a small knife, 15 to 20 minutes. Transfer the chicken to a plate and let rest for 5 minutes.

Meanwhile, pour the reserved vinaigrette into a small nonreactive saucepan and bring it to a boil. Remove from the heat and set aside.

To serve, slice the breasts crosswise on an angle and fan the slices on individual plates. Bring the vinaigrette back to a boil and pour over the chicken. Sprinkle with the sesame seeds.

Chicken Cutlets with Red Pepper Sauce

Serves 4

Water Level: Medium

You can also serve this simple, brilliant orange-red sauce with Chicken Breasts Stuffed Under the Skin with Rosemary Butter (page 97), or with steamed tuna or swordfish.

RED PEPPER SAUCE

1 red bell pepper, halved, cored, seeded, and ribs removed
2 tablespoons olive oil
$1/4$ teaspoon salt
$1/8$ teaspoon freshly ground black pepper

4 boneless, skinless chicken breast halves (1 to $1\frac{1}{4}$ pounds total)
Salt
1 tablespoon chopped flat-leaf parsley (optional)

For the sauce, put the pepper halves in the steaming basket, cover, and steam until tender, about 15 minutes. Transfer to a blender or food processor, add the remaining sauce ingredients, and puree until smooth.

Sprinkle the chicken with salt and place in a single layer in the steaming basket. Cover and steam until the chicken is cooked through and the juices run clear when the thickest part is pierced with a small knife, 15 to 20 minutes. Transfer to a plate and let rest for 5 minutes.

To serve, divide the sauce among four individual plates and spread it into an oval pool with the back of a spoon. Slice the breasts crosswise on an angle and fan over the sauce. Sprinkle with the parsley if using, and serve.

Chicken Fajitas

Serves 4
Water Level: Medium

You can make this recipe with steak as well; see the recipe on page 114 for the steaming time. I heat the tortillas individually in a nonstick frying pan, but you can also warm a stack of them, wrapped in foil, in a 325°F oven for fifteen minutes.

GUACAMOLE

1 ripe avocado, halved, pitted, and peeled
1/4 cup strained good-quality store-bought salsa
2 teaspoons fresh lime juice
1 teaspoon chopped fresh coriander

4 boneless, skinless chicken breast halves (1 to 1 1/4 pounds total)
Salt
1 lime, cut in half
1 red bell pepper, halved, cored, seeded, and ribs removed
6 to 8 slices (about 1/4 inch thick) red onion
8 flour tortillas

For the guacamole, mash the avocado with a fork in a shallow bowl until soft but still chunky. Stir in the salsa, lime juice, and coriander. Scrape into a serving bowl.

Sprinkle the chicken with salt and put it in a single layer in the steaming basket. Squeeze the juice of the lime over and put the pepper halves on top. Cover and steam for 15 minutes. Remove the bell pepper and pierce the thickest part of the chicken with a small knife: If the juices run clear, it's done; if not, cover and steam for 3 to 5 minutes longer.

Transfer the chicken to a plate and let rest for 5 minutes.

Add the onion slices to the steamer, cover, and steam for 5 minutes.

Cut the chicken crosswise into thin slices. Cut the pepper into 1-inch-wide strips. Place the chicken, pepper, and onion slices on a serving plate.

To warm the tortillas, heat a large nonstick pan over high heat. Add a tortilla and cook until it puffs slightly and begins to brown, about 45 seconds. Flip it, and heat for 15 to 30 seconds longer. Remove from the frying pan and heat the remaining tortillas in the same way, stacking them on a plate.

Let everyone make his or her own fajitas by stuffing the tortillas with the chicken, onions, peppers, and guacamole.

Chicken Breasts Stuffed Under the Skin with Rosemary Butter

Serves 2

Water Level: High (Medium if using the Waring)

A rosemary-flavored butter stuffed under the skin of the chicken breast flavors the meat as well as keeping it moist. You can use the leftover rosemary stem (or stems) and a few more stems with leaves as a bed for the chicken to add even more flavor during steaming. If you're not worried about fat, double the recipe for the butter; spread half of it under the skin and serve the remainder in dollops on top of the sliced chicken. The butter makes a sauce as it melts over the warm chicken. Or serve the chicken with the Red Pepper Sauce on page 95.

Save the juices in the drip pan (or reservoir if using the Waring) for soups or rice dishes (see page 92).

ROSEMARY BUTTER

1 tablespoon butter, at room temperature
$^{1}/_{2}$ teaspoon chopped fresh rosemary, stem(s) reserved,
    or $^{1}/_{4}$ teaspoon dried
Pinch of salt, or more to taste
Pinch of freshly ground black pepper, or more to taste

1 whole chicken breast on the bone (about $1^{1}/_{4}$ pounds)
Salt
2 sprigs fresh rosemary (optional)

continued

In a small bowl, mash the butter with the rosemary, salt, and pepper. Taste for seasoning.

Loosen the skin on the chicken breast without detaching it entirely, and rub the butter all over the flesh under the skin. Sprinkle the chicken all over with salt.

Place the reserved rosemary stem(s) and the sprigs, if using, in the steaming basket and place the chicken on top, skin side down. Cover and steam until the juices run clear when the thickest part of the chicken is pierced with a small knife, about 30 minutes. Set the steaming basket on a plate and let the chicken rest, covered, for 5 minutes. (Save any juices that collect on the plate along with the juices from the drip pan or reservoir.)

Cut the chicken off the bone in thin slices and serve.

Chicken Salad with Ginger, Red Pepper, and Snow Peas

Serves 2

Water Level: High (Medium if using the Waring)

Steamed white chicken meat is particularly good cold—the flesh relaxes and becomes velvety tender and moist. I like to steam the chicken several hours (or even a day) ahead, chill it, and then dress it with this ginger-sesame vinaigrette just before serving. If you don't have time to chill the chicken, the salad is fine served warm or at room temperature.

This vinaigrette is also tasty with leftover cooked beef.

1 whole chicken breast on the bone (about 1¼ pounds)
Salt
1 cup snow peas, cut in half on the diagonal
½ red bell pepper, cored, seeded, ribs removed, and cut in half
lengthwise and then crosswise into thin strips
Soy-Orange Vinaigrette (page 93)
1 teaspoon toasted sesame seeds

Sprinkle the chicken with salt and place it, skin side down, in the steaming basket. Cover and steam until the juices run clear when the thickest part of the chicken is pierced with a small knife, about 30 minutes. Remove to a plate to cool, then refrigerate until chilled.

Meanwhile spread the snow peas in the steaming basket, cover, and steam for 5 minutes. Leaving the snow peas in the basket, refresh under cold running water. Drain and pat dry, then cover and refrigerate.

Pull off the chicken skin. Cut down the breast bone to divide the breast in half, and pull and cut the two breast halves off the bone. Cut the breasts crosswise on the diagonal into ¼-inch-thick slices and put them in a bowl. Add the snow peas, red pepper strips, vinaigrette, and sesame seeds and toss gently to coat the chicken and vegetables.

Curried Chicken Salad

Serves 2

Water Level: (Medium if using the Waring

A couple of tablespoons of low-fat yogurt in place of some of the mayonnaise make this salad lower in fat than traditional chicken salads, and the acidity of the yogurt enhances the sweet grapes and coconut. Curry powders vary in strength; taste the mayonnaise and add more if it needs it.

1 whole chicken breast on the bone (about 1¹/₄ pounds)
Salt
2 small zucchini, trimmed

CURRY MAYONNAISE

¹/₃ cup mayonnaise, homemade (page 24) or store-bought regular
** or low-fat**
2 tablespoons plain, low-fat yogurt
1 tablespoon fresh lime juice
2 teaspoons curry powder, or more to taste
¹/₂ teaspoon grated fresh ginger (see headnote, page 61)
Salt and freshly ground black pepper to taste

10 seedless red grapes, cut in half, or scant ¹/₄ cup raisins
2 to 3 cups torn mixed lettuces
2 tablespoons sweetened shredded coconut, toasted in a frying pan over
** medium heat until lightly browned (about 1 minute)**
2 tablespoons slivered almonds, toasted in a frying pan until fragrant and
** golden (about 2 minutes)**

Sprinkle the chicken with salt. Put the chicken and zucchini in the steaming basket, cover, and steam for 20 minutes. Transfer the zucchini to a plate and refrigerate. Continue steaming the chicken until the juices run clear when the thickest part is pierced with a small knife, about 10 minutes longer. Remove the chicken from the steamer, cover, and refrigerate until cold, 1 to 2 hours.

Meanwhile, for the mayonnaise, stir together all the ingredients. Taste for salt and pepper. Cover and refrigerate until ready to use.

Pull off the chicken skin, cut down the breast bone to divide the breast in half, and cut and pull the two breast halves off the bone. Cut the meat into 1/2-inch chunks, and put it in a medium bowl. Cut the zucchini into 1/2-inch chunks.

Add the mayonnaise to the chicken and stir gently to coat the chicken. Gently fold in the zucchini and grapes or raisins.

To serve, make a bed of lettuce on two individual plates. Mound the salad on the lettuce and sprinkle with the coconut and almonds.

Cornish Game Hens Stuffed with Provençal Herbs

Serves 2
Water Level: High (Low if using the Waring)

Cornish game hens are perfect for the electric steamer: Steamed whole birds have more flavor than steamed parts and game hens are small enough to fit comfortably in these small steamers, whereas a whole chicken will not. Here the cavities are stuffed with a typical Provençal mixture of herbs, but you can use almost any herb; fresh tarragon, sage, or oregano. If you serve the hens with Ratatouille (page 47), you'll accentuate the provençal flavors of both, and you won't need a sauce. While the birds steam, they make an herb-flavored broth in the drip pan (or Waring's water reservoir). Use this broth in soups and rice dishes (see page 92). Or use some of it to make a sauce for the chicken (see Note).

2 Cornish game hens (about 1½ pounds each)
Salt
2 bay leaves
4 large sprigs fresh thyme
1 rosemary sprig, cut in half
Freshly ground black pepper

Pull the giblets, if any, out of the cavities of the hens. Discard the livers and put the gizzards and hearts in the drip pan, or in the reservoir if using the Waring, to flavor the juices. Rinse the hens, pat them dry, and sprinkle the cavities with salt. Stuff each cavity with a bay leaf, half the thyme, and half the rosemary branch. Put the hens in the steaming basket, cover, and steam until the juices run clear when the thighs are pierced with a small knife, 35 to 40 minutes. If using a steamer with a drip pan, check it after 10 minutes and then once more during the steaming time; pour the juices off into a bowl as it fills, leaving the giblets in the tray (see Equipment Notes).

Set the steaming basket on a plate and let the hens rest, covered, for 5 minutes.

Meanwhile, pour the juices remaining in the drip pan into the bowl (above), or, if using the Waring, pour the juices from the reservoir into a bowl. Discard the gizzards and hearts (eat the gizzards if you like). Add any juices from the plate on which the hens are resting to the bowl. Use the broth to make a sauce for the hens (see Note), or cool and refrigerate for another use.

Serve the hens whole, or split them down the breastbones with a large knife or kitchen scissors and cut along either side of the backbone to remove it. Pull off the skin if you like. Put each hen on a plate, grind pepper over, and serve.

• **Equipment Notes:** If using the Rival, use a bulb baster to empty the drip pan. If using the West Bend, don't wait until the pan is full to empty it; it is very difficult to handle when full of boiling-hot liquid, and you don't want to lose any of the broth.

• **Note:** If you like, you can use some of the steaming liquid to make a light, brothy sauce for the hens: Skim off the fat and reduce half a cup of the broth by half in a small saucepan. Whisk one to two tablespoons cold butter bit by bit into the boiling broth, and serve with the birds.

Cornish Game Hens with Mushrooms

Serves 2

Water Level: High (Low if using the Waring)

This recipe uses the steaming juices from the birds in a mushroom sauce. The easiest way to defat the juices is with one of these plastic degreasing cups, sold in kitchenware stores. If you don't have a degreasing cup, bring the juices to a simmer in a saucepan and skim the fat that rises to the surface with a ladle. This takes a bit more time, but it'll do the trick.

Although I often leave the skin on steamed poultry, I pull it off for this recipe because the sauce coats the bird better without it.

A hen, with the mushroom sauce, pretty much fills a standard dinner plate. Here's a place where it makes sense to serve the vegetable as a first course: perhaps Celery with Olive Oil, Lemon, and Parmesan (page 36), Green Beans with Walnuts and Sherry Vinegar (page 27), or stuffed artichokes (pages 20–23).

If you have an open bottle of white wine, it makes for a particularly refined sauce. If not, don't worry; the juices give the sauce enough flavor without the wine.

2 Cornish game hens (about 1¹/₂ pounds each)
8 large pieces dried porcini mushrooms (about ¹/₃ ounce)
Salt

MUSHROOM SAUCE

1 tablespoon butter
1 tablespoon olive oil
¹/₂ pound assorted fresh mushrooms, thinly sliced, such as white, shiitake, cremini, and oyster, trimmed (shiitake stems removed)
1 shallot, minced
¹/₂ teaspoon salt, or more to taste
2 tablespoons white wine (optional)
1¹/₂ to 2 cups reserved steaming juices (see above)
1 tablespoon chopped flat-leaf parsley
¹/₂ teaspoon chopped fresh tarragon (optional)
¹/₈ teaspoon freshly ground black pepper

Freshly ground black pepper

Pull the giblets, if any, out of the cavities of the hens. Discard the livers and put the gizzards and hearts in the drip pan, or in the water reservoir if using the Waring. Add the dried mushrooms. Rinse the hens, pat them dry, and sprinkle the cavities with salt.

Place the hens in the steaming basket, cover, and steam until the juices run clear when the thighs are pierced with a small knife, 35 to 40 minutes. If using a steamer with a drip pan, check it after 10 minutes and then once more during the steaming time; pour the juices off into a bowl as it fills, leaving the giblets and mushrooms in the pan (see Equipment Notes). Set the bowl aside.

Meanwhile, for the sauce, heat the butter and oil in a large frying pan over high heat until very hot. Add the mushrooms and sauté until lightly browned, 8 to 10 minutes. Add the shallot and salt and sauté until translucent, about 2 minutes. Add the white wine, if using, and cook until most of the wine has evaporated. Remove from the heat and set aside.

Set the steaming basket on a plate and let the birds rest, covered, while you finish the sauce. Remove the dried mushrooms from the drip pan or reservoir, chop, and add to the sautéed mushrooms. Pour all the juices from the drip pan, or the juices from the reservoir if using the Waring, into a degreasing cup, then pour the juices into the frying pan (leaving the fat in the cup). Bring to a boil over high heat and boil until reduced and thickened. Stir in the parsley, the tarragon, if using, and the pepper. Taste for salt.

To serve, split the hens down the breastbones with a large knife or kitchen scissors and cut along either side of the backbone to remove it. Pull off the skin if you like. Spoon the sauce onto individual plates and place the birds on top. Grind pepper over and serve.

• **Equipment Notes:** If using the Rival, use a bulb baster to empty the drip pan. If using the West Bend, don't wait until the drip pan is full to empty it; it is very difficult to handle when full of boiling-hot liquid, and you don't want to lose any of the broth.

Turkey Pita Pockets

Serves 4

Water Level: High

This cumin-flavored turkey meat loaf is delicious stuffed into pita breads and garnished with tomatoes, cucumber, and the yogurt sauce. It's good hot or at room temperature, or serve it as a traditional meat loaf, with the sauce. The recipe makes enough to serve four comfortably, with leftovers.

One 10-ounce package frozen spinach
2 pounds ground turkey
1 medium onion, coarsely grated (about $1/2$ cup)
1 tablespoon chopped flat-leaf parsley
2 teaspoons ground cumin
$1/2$ teaspoon dried oregano
1 teaspoon salt
$1/8$ teaspoon freshly ground black pepper

MINT-YOGURT SAUCE

1 cup low-fat plain yogurt
2 tablespoons fresh lemon juice
1 teaspoon chopped fresh mint
1 teaspoon salt

2 medium tomatoes, cored and cut into $1/4$- to $1/2$-inch-thick slices
1 medium cucumber, peeled and cut into $1/4$-inch-thick slices
4 pita breads

Put the spinach in the steaming basket, cover, and steam for 15 minutes to defrost. Leaving the spinach in the basket, refresh it under cold running water. Squeeze between your hands to remove as much water as possible.

Combine the turkey, onion, spinach, parsley, cumin, oregano, salt, and pepper in a bowl and mix well with your hands or a fork. Mound the mixture into the steaming basket, shaping it roughly into a 4-inch-wide and 3-inch-high round loaf. Cover and steam for 40 minutes, or until the internal temperature reaches 155°F.

Meanwhile, whisk together all of the sauce ingredients in a small bowl. Refrigerate until ready to serve.

Preheat the oven to 350°F.

When the meat loaf is cooked, set the steaming basket on a plate or in the sink and let stand, covered, for 5 minutes, or until the internal temperature reaches 165°F.

Meanwhile, warm the pita breads in the oven for about 5 minutes.

To serve, cut off the top inch of each bread and stuff it into the bottom of the pocket. Cut four 1- to 1½-inch-thick slices of the turkey loaf and stuff into the pockets. Add the tomato and cucumber slices and spoon in the sauce.

Kasha-Stuffed Turkey Cutlets with Zucchini

Serves 2
Water Level: Medium (Low if using the Waring)

Kasha, or roasted buckwheat groats, has a distinctive, earthy grain flavor that is just the right counterpoint for mild-flavored turkey. You can also serve the kasha on its own, to accompany poultry, meat, or fish. The three quarters of a cup of water is just enough liquid to cook the kasha if the heat is very low and the pan has a tight-fitting lid; use a heavy-bottomed pan, or a heat diffuser if you have one. Stuff the cutlets as soon as the kasha is cooked so that the kasha mixture doesn't dry out.

Depending on the brand, turkey cutlets are packaged differently. Some have four regular slices of equal thickness per package, while others are cut in less regular pieces. Pound the cutlets with the back of a large knife or a meat tenderizer if they are thick, and piece together smaller pieces as necessary to come up with four cutlets of about the same size.

continued

sour cream adds body but doesn't change the flavor of the sauce appreciably.

KASHA STUFFING

2 tablespoons butter
$^1/_4$ cup chopped onion
$^1/_4$ teaspoon salt
4 large white mushrooms, trimmed and chopped (about $1^1/_2$ cups)
$^1/_2$ cup medium-grind kasha
$^3/_4$ cup water

4 turkey cutlets (slightly less than 1 pound total)
Salt and freshly ground black pepper
1 medium zucchini, trimmed, halved lengthwise, seeds scooped out
**   with a spoon, and halves cut in half crosswise**

Mushroom Sauce

1 tablespoon butter
4 large white mushrooms, trimmed and thinly sliced
1 scallion, chopped
Salt
Reserved steaming liquid from turkey (see above)
$^1/_4$ cup low-fat plain yogurt
Freshly ground black pepper

For the kasha, melt the butter in a small heavy saucepan over medium-low heat. Add the onion and salt, cover, and cook, without coloring, until translucent, about 5 minutes. Add the mushrooms, cover, and cook until tender, about 5 minutes. Stir in the kasha, add the water, and bring to a simmer. Reduce the heat to as low as possible, cover tightly, and cook for 10 minutes. Remove from the heat and let stand for 5 minutes.

Lay one of the turkey cutlets on a work surface, and sprinkle lightly with salt and pepper. Spread $^1/_4$ cup of the kasha mixture over the meat and loosely roll up the cutlet, starting at a narrow end. Place seam side down in the steaming basket, and repeat with the remaining cutlets.

down in the steaming basket, and repeat with the remaining cutlets. Cover the remaining kasha mixture and set aside. Tuck the zucchini quarters into the basket, cover, and steam until the turkey is cooked through, about 20 minutes.

Meanwhile, for the sauce, melt the butter in a medium saucepan over medium heat. Add the mushrooms, scallion, and a pinch of salt, cover, and cook until the mushrooms give up their juices, about 5 minutes. Remove from the heat and set aside.

When the turkey is cooked, set the covered steaming basket on a plate or in the sink. (Reserve the steaming juices in the drip pan or reservoir.)

Stuff the zucchini quarters with the remaining kasha mixture. Replace them in the steaming basket and let stand, covered, while you finish the sauce. (The residual heat in the basket is sufficient to rewarm the kasha.)

Pour the steaming juices from the drip pan (there should be about ¾ cup), or ¾ cup of the liquid from the reservoir if using the Waring, into the pan with the mushrooms. Bring to a boil and boil until reduced by about half, 4 to 5 minutes. Remove from the heat and stir in the yogurt. Add salt, if needed, and pepper to taste.

To serve, put two stuffed cutlets and two zucchini halves on each plate. Spoon the sauce over.

• **Equipment Notes:** If using the Rival, use a bulb baster to empty the drip pan.

Steamed Duck

Although duck may seem an unlikely candidate for the steamer, you'll find that steaming leaves the lean breast moist and the legs melt-in-your-mouth tender. Since a whole duck won't fit in the steamer, I give separate recipes for boneless breast pieces and legs to be served at different meals. It's unlikely that you'll be able to find legs and breasts sold separately; buy the whole duck and have the butcher cut it up to give you two legs and two boneless breast pieces. Save the carcass for a stock or soup. If you like duck fat, render it by cutting all the fat and skin off the duck carcass and putting it in a large saucepan with about a quarter cup of water. Simmer over low heat until the fat is clear. Strain and refrigerate. Use the fat to sauté potatoes or greens or to flavor soups and stews.

The recipe calls for steaming the legs until the meat is almost falling off the bone and much of the fat has been rendered. Then the skin is browned under the broiler. Serve the duck legs with sautéed potatoes, lentils, Cabbage in Bacon Cream Sauce (page 34), Sautéed Spinach with Garlic and Lemon (page 46), or Ratatouille (page 47). Save the steaming juices for the duck breast recipe.

The breast pieces are steamed medium-rare, the skin is removed (the skin doesn't render enough of its fat during the short steaming time to make it pleasant to eat), and the meat is sliced and served with a spicy, saucy vegetable stew made with the reserved steaming juices from the legs. If a quarter of a duck seems skimpy, serve each person half a duck: Steam the legs first, then make the vegetable stew and steam the breast pieces while you broil the legs.

Duck Legs Steamed on a Bed of Thyme

Serves 2

Water Level: High (Medium if using the Waring)

The fresh thyme is something of a luxury here; it's delicious with duck but not absolutely necessary. You can broil the legs or finish them in a cast-iron grill pan, on top of the stove.

2 duck legs (about 10 ounces each)
Salt
$^1\!/_2$ bunch fresh thyme (optional)
Freshly ground black pepper

Prick the skin and the fatty deposits on the meaty insides of the legs with a sharp-pronged fork. Sprinkle lightly all over with salt. Make a bed of the thyme, if using, in the steaming basket and put the legs on top. Cover and steam until the meat is very tender, about 1 hour and 15 minutes. Check the drip pan often during steaming and empty it into a bowl as it fills, reserving the liquid; or, if using the Waring, check the water level in the reservoir halfway through the steaming time (see Equipment Notes).

Preheat the broiler.

When the legs are cooked, take them out of the steaming basket, reserving the juices in the drip pan or reservoir. Broil the legs, skin side up, until the skin is golden brown and crisp, about 5 minutes. Turn the legs over and broil for a few minutes longer. Grind pepper over and serve hot.

Defat the steaming juices in a degreasing cup or in a saucepan, using a ladle (see headnote, page 104). Or refrigerate until chilled; the fat will rise to the surface and can be skimmed off easily. Use the juices in the recipe on page 112.

continued

• **Equipment Notes:** If using the Rival, use a bulb baster to empty the drip pan. If using the West Bend, don't wait until the pan is full to empty it; it gets very difficult to handle when full of boiling-hot liquid and you don't want to lose any of the broth. If using the Waring, you may need to empty the juices from the reservoir once and refill the reservoir with fresh water.

Duck Breasts with Kale, Corn, and Tomatoes

Serves 2
Water Level: Medium

Serve this with bread or warm tortillas. If you like, substitute 2 packed cups torn Swiss chard leaves for the kale.

KALE AND CORN STEW

2 tablespoons olive oil
1 medium onion
$\frac{1}{2}$ large jalapeño pepper, seeded, ribs removed, and thinly sliced crosswise (seeds left in if you like spicy food)
$\frac{1}{2}$ teaspoon salt
2 plum tomatoes, cored and coarsely chopped
1 cup fresh (from 1 ear) or thawed frozen corn kernels
2 reserved cups duck steaming juices from duck legs (see page 111), chicken stock or canned low-sodium broth, or steaming juices from chicken or Cornish game hen
4 large leaves kale, washed and torn into 2-inch pieces (about 2 packed cups)
1 tablespoon red wine vinegar

2 boneless duck breast halves (7 to 8 ounces each)
Salt

For the stew, heat the olive oil in a large frying pan over medium heat. Add the onion, jalapeño, and $\frac{1}{4}$ teaspoon of the salt and cook, stirring often, until the onion is tender and beginning to brown, about 10 minutes. Add the tomatoes and corn and cook, stirring, for about 2 minutes. Add the duck juices or stock and bring to a simmer. Add the kale, vinegar, and the remaining $\frac{1}{4}$ teaspoon salt, cover, reduce the heat to medium-low, and simmer until the kale is tender but still has some bite and the juices have reduced and thickened slightly, about 15 minutes. Check occasionally to see that the juices aren't evaporating too quickly; if the pan is getting dry, turn down the heat or add a little water.

Meanwhile, sprinkle the meat side of the duck breasts with salt and put them skin side down in the steaming basket. Cover and steam until medium-rare, about 15 minutes. Set the steaming basket on a plate and let rest, covered, for 5 minutes. Then pull and cut off the skin and discard (or reserve to render for fat). Slice the breasts crosswise on an angle, and pour any juices that have collected on the plate into the kale and corn stew.

To serve, spoon the vegetable mixture onto individual plates. Fan the duck on top.

Serve with bread or warm tortillas.

Marinated Steak with Tomatoes and Balsamic Vinegar

Serves 2
Water Level: Medium

Steamed steak sounds unusual, I'll grant you, but try this—you'll be amazed at the pure flavor of the meat. The steak gives off its juices into the marinade and so makes a sauce while it steams.

<u>MARINADE</u>

2 tablespoons olive oil
3 tablespoons balsamic vinegar
2 plum tomatoes, cored and chopped
1 medium shallot, thinly sliced
1 teaspoon chopped fresh thyme

1 pound London broil, about 1¼ inches thick
Salt and freshly ground black pepper

Aluminum foil

For the marinade, combine all the ingredients in a shallow baking dish. Add the beef and turn to coat. Cover and marinate in the refrigerator for at least 2 hours, or overnight.

Put the beef in the rice bowl and sprinkle with salt. Pour the marinade over and cover with aluminum foil. Place in the steaming basket, cover, and steam until the meat is medium-rare, about 30 minutes (see Equipment Notes). Let rest for 5 minutes.

Thinly slice the beef and place on individual plates. Grind pepper over and spoon the marinade on top. Serve with baked, steamed, or boiled potatoes or rice or bread to sop up the sauce.

• **Equipment Notes:** The Waring doesn't have a rice bowl large enough to hold the steak; marinate the steak and then steam it in the steaming basket. Bring the marinade to a boil in a saucepan to serve with the steak. If using the Rival steamer, put the rice bowl directly on the steamer base, as described in the instruction manual.

Meatballs with Tomato Sauce

Serves 2
Water Level: Medium

A low-fat rendition of an old favorite.

TOMATO SAUCE

One 16-ounce can Italian plum tomatoes, drained, $\frac{1}{2}$ cup juices reserved
2 tablespoons olive oil
1 tablespoon chopped flat-leaf parsley
$\frac{1}{2}$ teaspoon sugar
$\frac{1}{8}$ teaspoon dried oregano
$\frac{1}{4}$ teaspoon salt, or more to taste
$\frac{1}{8}$ teaspoon freshly ground black pepper, or more to taste

MEATBALLS

$\frac{3}{4}$ cup lean ground beef (such as round)
$\frac{1}{4}$ cup chopped onion
$\frac{1}{2}$ cup cooked rice
1 tablespoon chopped flat-leaf parsley
$\frac{3}{4}$ teaspoon salt
$\frac{1}{4}$ teaspoon allspice
$\frac{1}{8}$ teaspoon freshly ground black pepper
6 dashes of Tabasco sauce, or to taste (optional)

For the sauce, cut off the core ends of the tomatoes. Coarsely chop the tomatoes and put them with the reserved $\frac{1}{2}$ cup juices in a medium saucepan. Add the remaining sauce ingredients and bring to a simmer. Simmer gently, uncovered, until the sauce has reduced by about one quarter, about 15 minutes. Remove from the heat.

Meanwhile, for the meatballs, combine all the ingredients in a medium bowl and mix with your hands or a fork to combine. Shape the mixture into 8 balls and put them in a single layer in the steaming basket. Cover and steam until just cooked through, about 15 minutes.

To serve, return the sauce to a simmer. Taste and adjust the seasoning. Using a large spoon, carefully transfer the meatballs to a serving bowl. Pour the sauce over and serve.

Beef Shin "Pot-au-Feu"

Serves 2 generously

Water Level: High (Medium if using the Waring)

This is an adaptation of a traditional French pot-au-feu, in which meat and vegetables are poached together in a broth. Unlike the original, this version requires very little cooking skill and almost no surveillance. And it's one of the best things I've ever eaten. Beef shin (on a calf this same cut is called a veal shank) is underused, although I can't imagine why; it's got tremendous flavor and luscious texture, and the marrow to boot. The sauce, a sherry vinegar vinaigrette green with capers and parsley, is dynamite with the beef as well as with all the vegetables. Leftovers (and there almost certainly will be some) are delicious the next day. Ask the butcher to tie the shins around the outside with a piece of string to keep the meat together and to make it easy to get them in and out of the steamer.

2 slices beef shin (1$\frac{1}{4}$ to 1$\frac{1}{2}$ pounds each), cut 1$\frac{3}{4}$ inches thick

Salt

2 medium carrots, peeled, trimmed, and cut in half lengthwise and then in half crosswise

1 medium turnip, peeled, trimmed, and cut into 8 wedges

2 inner celery stalks, trimmed, peeled deeply with a small knife to remove the strings, and cut in half crosswise

5 to 6 tiny new potatoes, cut in half, or 3 medium new potatoes, quartered

PARSLEY-CAPER SAUCE

1 tablespoon sherry vinegar

$\frac{1}{4}$ teaspoon salt

3 tablespoons olive oil

1 large shallot, chopped

1 tablespoon drained small capers, chopped

2 tablespoons chopped flat-leaf parsley

$\frac{1}{8}$ teaspoon freshly ground black pepper

Freshly ground black pepper
Dijon mustard
Coarse salt (optional)

Sprinkle the shin pieces all over with salt and put them in a single layer in the steaming basket. Cover and steam for 1 hour. Check the drip pan, or the water reservoir if using the Waring, at least once during steaming and pour the juices into a medium saucepan (see Equipment Notes).

Add all the vegetables to the steaming basket and steam until the meat is very tender and the vegetables are tender when pierced with a small knife, about 25 minutes longer.

Meanwhile, for the sauce, whisk together the vinegar and salt. Whisk in the olive oil and then the remaining ingredients.

When the meat and vegetables are cooked, set the steaming basket on a plate and let stand, covered, while you reduce the broth.

Pour the broth remaining in the drip pan or the reservoir into the saucepan (above) and bring to a simmer. Skim the fat from the broth with a ladle or a large spoon, bring to a boil, and boil until reduced to ¾ to 1 cup.

To serve, put the beef on deep individual plates and cut off the strings. Grind pepper over. Arrange the vegetables around the shins and pour the broth over. Spoon the sauce over the meat or serve on the side, with bowls of mustard and the coarse salt, if using. Don't forget to dig out and eat the marrow from the center of the bones.

• **Equipment Notes:** If using the Waring, empty the reservoir into the saucepan as needed and refill the reservoir with fresh water. If using the Rival, use a bulb baster to empty the drip pan. If using the West Bend, don't wait until the pan is full to empty it; it is very difficult to handle when full of boiling-hot liquid, and you don't want to lose any of the broth.

Spice-Rubbed Pork Ribs

Serves 2

Water Level: High (Medium if using the Waring)

These ribs are rubbed with a spice mixture to season them during steaming. Serve the ribs with the vinegar sauce below, or the hearty Barbecue Sauce on page 120. This recipe uses what are called country-style ribs; they aren't true ribs at all, but rather chops cut from the rib end of the pork loin that are tasty, meaty, and fatty. Steaming the ribs renders much of this fat. (Spareribs work as well.)

This recipe makes one quarter cup of rub, about twice what you'll need for two pounds of ribs, but it'll keep forever in a cupboard. The sauce is spicy; cut the Tabasco to an eighth of a teaspoon if you don't like hot food.

CHILI RUB

2 tablespoons chili powder

1 tablespoon paprika

1 tablespoon ground cumin

1 tablespoon granulated sugar

1 tablespoon brown sugar

1 tablespoon freshly ground black pepper

2 teaspoons salt

1³/₄ to 2 pounds country-style pork ribs or pork spareribs

SWEET-AND-SOUR VINEGAR SAUCE

¹/₃ cup cider vinegar

2¹/₂ teaspoons sugar

¹/₄ teaspoon Tabasco sauce, or to taste

¹/₈ teaspoon salt

¹/₈ teaspoon freshly ground black pepper

Aluminum foil

For the rub, stir together all the ingredients in a bowl. Or put them in a large jar, cover, and shake to combine. Rub the ribs all over with about half of the rub (the object is not to cover the pork completely with the rub, like a flour coating, but to season the meat heavily).

Put the ribs in the steaming basket, layering them as necessary to fit, cover, and steam until the meat is tender and much of the fat has been rendered, about 1½ hours. Check the drip pan after the first 20 minutes, or the water level in the reservoir after 45 minutes to an hour if using the Waring; you'll need to empty the drip pan two to three times, or the reservoir at least once, during steaming (see Equipment Notes).

Meanwhile, preheat the oven to 450°F. Line a baking sheet with aluminum foil.

When the ribs are cooked, lay them on the prepared baking sheet. Bake for 5 to 10 minutes, until browned.

Whisk together all the sauce ingredients in a bowl. Brush the sauce over the ribs or serve it on the side.

• **Equipment Notes:** If using the Waring, empty the reservoir and refill with fresh water once or twice during steaming. If using the Rival, use a bulb baster to empty the drip pan. If using the West Bend, don't wait until the pan is full to empty it; it is difficult to handle when full of boiling-hot liquid.

Barbecued Baby Back Ribs

Serves 2

Water Level: High (Medium if using the Waring)

I make this recipe with the small pork ribs called baby back ribs, but pork spareribs or the meatier country-style ribs used in the recipe on page 118 work just as well. The sauce is a traditional sweet-and-sour ketchup-based American barbecue sauce.

continued

1 rack baby back pork ribs (about 2 pounds)

BARBECUE SAUCE

1 tablespoon canola oil
$^1/_2$ cup chopped onions
1 garlic clove, chopped
1 cup ketchup
$^1/_4$ cup cider vinegar
Juice of 1 large orange
2 tablespoons Dijon mustard
$^1/_4$ cup packed brown sugar
1 teaspoon chili powder
$^1/_4$ teaspoon ground cumin
$^1/_4$ teaspoon Tabasco sauce

Aluminum foil

Put the ribs in the steaming basket, bending or cutting them as necessary to fit, cover, and steam until the meat is tender and much of the fat has been rendered, about 1$^1/_2$ hours. Check the drip pan, or the reservoir if using the Waring, after the first 45 minutes and pour off the juices as necessary (see Equipment Notes); then check once more during steaming.

Meanwhile, make the sauce: Heat the oil in a medium saucepan over medium-low heat. Add the onions and garlic, cover, and cook, without browning, until translucent, about 5 minutes. Stir in all the remaining ingredients and simmer for about 10 minutes, until slightly reduced and thickened.

Preheat the oven to 450°F. Line a baking sheet with aluminum foil.

When the ribs are tender, put them on the prepared baking sheet and spoon the sauce over, turning the ribs to coat them with the sauce. Turn meaty sides up and bake for 10 to 15 minutes, until glazed.

• **Equipment Notes:** If using the Waring, empty the reservoir and refill with clean water once or twice during steaming. If using the Rival, use a bulb baster to empty the drip pan. If using the West Bend, don't wait until the pan is full to empty it; it is difficult to handle when full of boiling-hot liquid.

Lamb Riblets with Maple-Soy Glaze

Serves 2

Water Level: High (Medium if using the Waring)

Lamb riblets are a little-known cut, and that's too bad: They're heavenly and dirt-cheap. The lamb gives off a lot of fat as it steams, so you'll need to empty the drip pan or reservoir once or twice during steaming.

2$^{1}/_{2}$ to 3 pounds lamb riblets

MAPLE-SOY GLAZE

$^{1}/_{4}$ cup Dijon mustard
2 tablespoons soy sauce
2 teaspoons rice wine vinegar or cider vinegar
$^{1}/_{2}$ cup maple syrup

Aluminum foil

Layer the riblets in the steaming basket, bending them as necessary to fit, cover, and steam until the meat is tender and much of the fat has been rendered, about 1½ hours. Check the drip pan after the first half hour, or the water level in the reservoir after the first 45 minutes if using the Waring; you'll need to empty the drip pan two to three times, or empty the reservoir at least once, during steaming (see Equipment Notes).

Meanwhile, make the glaze: Whisk together the mustard, soy sauce, and vinegar, then whisk in the maple syrup.

Preheat the broiler. Line a baking sheet with aluminum foil.

Place the ribs on the baking sheet and spoon about half of the glaze over, turning the ribs to coat them. Turn the ribs meaty side up and broil, spooning more glaze over them half-way through the cooking time, until browned and caramelized, about 10 minutes. Serve hot.

• **Equipment Notes:** If using the Waring, empty the reservoir and refill with fresh water as necessary during steaming. If using the Rival, use a bulb baster to empty the drip pan. If using the West Bend, don't wait until the pan is full to empty it; it is difficult to handle when full of boiling-hot liquid.

Desserts

W hile the steamer isn't going to replace the oven when it comes to making cakes and cookies, it sure does when we want custards and puddings. Steaming is a foolproof method for making egg-based desserts usually cooked in a water bath to keep the eggs from curdling. And it's far easier than shuttling a heavy pan of boiling water in and out of the oven.

Custards are steamed in individual foil-covered ramekins or in custard cups; the recipes are for two because the steaming baskets aren't large enough to hold four cups. Steam in two batches if you need to. Bittersweet Chocolate Pudding Cake, Indian Pudding, and Lemon Cheesecake are steamed in slightly smaller cupcake aluminum cups made by EZ-Foil, and four of these do fit in the basket. The small cups make a pretty presentation, and these desserts are too rich to serve in larger quantities. Bread and rice puddings are exceptionally moist when steamed in the rice bowl. The bread puddings can be eaten straightaway or made several hours ahead, sliced, and warmed in the oven to give a light crust.

Simple fruit desserts, such as Peaches in Red Wine (page 140) and Chilled Apricots with Blueberries and Lime (page 144), are quick to make in the steamer and can be low in fat as well, if you choose.

Master Recipe for Vanilla Custard

Serves 2
Water Level: High

Custards, usually baked in a water bath to keep them from curdling, are blessedly easy to make in a steamer. Here is a simple vanilla custard made with milk and three variations, one using half-and-half. I've made custard in larger quantities and steamed it in the rice bowl, but single servings are more elegant and easier to serve.

Be careful not to overcook these custards. When cooked to perfection, the centers will still jiggle like Jell-O; don't be fooled into thinking they're underdone. If you're unsure, pierce the centers with the point of a knife; it should come out clean.

2 large eggs
¹/₄ cup sugar
²/₃ cup milk
¹/₂ teaspoon vanilla extract

2 Pyrex or porcelain custard cups, about 6 ounces each
Aluminum foil

In a medium bowl, whisk the eggs with the sugar until well mixed and light-colored. Whisk in the milk and vanilla, and pour into the custard cups. Cover each cup with a small square of aluminum foil, place in the steaming basket, cover, and steam until the custards are just set but still jiggle slightly in the center, about 20 minutes. Remove from the steamer and let cool for 5 minutes. Then refrigerate until chilled, about 2 hours.

VARIATIONS

Cinnamon–Brown Sugar Custard

2 large eggs
¼ cup packed brown sugar
⅔ cup milk
½ teaspoon vanilla extract
Ground cinnamon and freshly grated nutmeg for serving

2 Pyrex or porcelain custard cups, about 6 ounces each
Aluminum foil

Whisk together the eggs and sugar until well mixed and light-colored, then whisk in the milk and vanilla. Steam and chill the custards as directed in the Master Recipe. Sprinkle the chilled custards with cinnamon and nutmeg before serving.

Grand Marnier Custard

2 large eggs
¼ cup plus 1 tablespoon sugar
2 tablespoons Grand Marnier
Grated zest of 1 orange
⅔ cup milk

2 Pyrex or porcelain custard cups, about 6 ounces each
Aluminum foil

Whisk the eggs with the sugar, Grand Marnier, and zest until well mixed and light-colored, then whisk in the milk. Steam and chill as directed in the Master Recipe.

Coffee Custard

²/₃ cup half-and-half
³/₄ teaspoon instant espresso powder, preferably Medaglio d'Oro
2 large eggs
¹/₄ cup sugar
¹/₂ teaspoon vanilla extract

Stir together the half-and-half and espresso in a small bowl to dissolve the espresso. In a medium bowl, whisk together the eggs and sugar until well mixed and light-colored, then whisk in the half-and-half mixture and the vanilla. Steam and chill the custards as directed in the Master Recipe.

Rich Chocolate Custard

Serves 2
Water Level: High

A little cinnamon in this custard makes it taste like what I knew as a kid as Mexican hot chocolate; it enhances chocolate's spicy bitterness, usually hidden under its sweetness. The steamer is an easy way to melt chocolate.

²/₃ **cup half-and-half**
1¹/₄ **ounces good-quality bittersweet chocolate, such as Lindt,**
   coarsely chopped
2 large eggs
2 tablespoons sugar
¹/₂ **teaspoon vanilla extract**
¹/₄ **teaspoon cinnamon (optional)**

Pyrex or porcelain custard cups, about 6 ounces each
Aluminum foil

Combine the half-and-half and chocolate in the rice bowl (do not cover with aluminum foil). Place in the steaming basket (see Equipment Notes), cover, and steam until the chocolate melts, 10 to 15 minutes (or combine in a small saucepan and heat over low heat until the chocolate melts).

In a medium bowl, whisk together the eggs and sugar until well mixed and light-colored, then whisk in the chocolate mixture. Whisk in the vanilla and the cinnamon, if using. Pour the mixture into the custard cups. Cover each cup with a small square of foil, place in the steaming basket, cover, and steam until the custards are just set but still jiggle slightly in the center, about 18 minutes; the blade of a small knife should come out gooey. Remove from the steamer and let cool for 5 minutes. Then refrigerate until chilled, about 2 hours.

• **Equipment Notes:** If using the Rival or Waring steamers, put the rice bowl directly on the steamer base, as described in the instruction manuals, rather than in the steaming basket.

Orange Pudding

Serves 2
Water Level: Medium

This pudding has a particularly fresh sweet and tart orange taste because it's made with orange and lemon juice, without any milk or cream. Serve it hot from the steamer or cold, with whipped cream if you like.

$1/2$ **cup fresh orange juice (about 1 medium orange)**
1 teaspoon cornstarch
Juice of 1 lemon
$1/4$ **cup sugar**
2 large eggs
Sweetened whipped cream for serving (optional)

2 Pyrex or porcelain custard cups, about 6 ounces each
Aluminum foil

Stir together 1 tablespoon of the orange juice and the cornstarch in a small bowl.

Combine the remaining orange juice, the lemon juice, and sugar in a saucepan and heat, stirring over medium heat until the sugar just dissolves; (don't allow the juice to boil). Give the cornstarch mixture a stir, whisk it into the juice, and cook, whisking, for a few seconds, until the mixture thickens. Remove from the heat.

Whisk the eggs in a medium bowl until well mixed and frothy. Whisking constantly, gradually add a few tablespoons of the hot juice mixture to temper the eggs, then whisk in the rest of the juice mixture.

Pour the mixture into the custard cups and cover each with a square of aluminum foil. Place the cups in the steaming basket, cover, and steam until the puddings are set, about 20 minutes. Serve hot, or refrigerate until chilled and serve cold, with whipped cream if desired.

Indian Corn Pudding

Serves 4
Water Level: High

Sweet and spicy with molasses, cinnamon, and ginger, this creamy golden pudding is delicious cold, but even better hot or warm. It has enough cornmeal to give the pudding texture without making it dense, and the molasses spills out of the pudding to make a sauce, like a crème caramel.

Traditionally, the cornmeal is cooked in a saucepan on top of the stove, then mixed with other ingredients and steamed, but you can do the whole process in the rice bowl of the steamer. I use Grandma's Molasses, the unsulfured and mild-flavored version, because the flavor doesn't overwhelm the pudding. The puddings are steamed in four-ounce aluminum cupcake cups made by EZ-Foil, sold in kitchenware and hardware stores; four fit easily into any of the steamers.

$1^1/_2$ **cups milk**
$^1/_4$ **cup yellow cornmeal**
$^1/_2$ **cup molasses**
4 tablespoons unsalted butter
$^1/_2$ **teaspoon cinnamon**
$^1/_4$ **teaspoon powdered ginger**
$^1/_4$ **teaspoon salt**
1 large egg

Softened butter for the cupcake cups

Aluminum foil
Four 4-ounce aluminum cupcake cups (see headnote)

Grease the cupcake cups with softened butter.

Pour the milk into the rice bowl (do not cover with foil), place the rice bowl in the steaming basket (see Equipment Notes), cover, and steam until the milk is hot, 17 to 20 minutes. Stir in the cornmeal, cover, and steam, stirring occasionally, until slightly thickened, about 20 minutes. Stir in the molasses, cover, and steam for 3 minutes. Remove the rice bowl from the steamer and whisk in the butter, spices, salt, and egg.

Divide the pudding mixture among the buttered cupcake cups, cover each with a square of aluminum foil, and put them in the steaming basket. Cover and steam until the custard is set, about 30 minutes. Remove the cups from the steamer and let stand for 5 minutes. Turn out onto individual plates and serve hot or warm, or chill and serve cold.

• **Equipment Notes:** If using the Rival or Waring steamers, put the rice bowl directly on the steamer base, as described in the instruction manuals, rather than in the steaming basket.

Bittersweet Chocolate Pudding Cake

Serves 4
Water Level: High

This rich but not-too-sweet cake is steamed until the sides are just set, like a moist brownie, but the center is still soft, so it runs out of the cake when you cut into it.

6 ounces good-quality bittersweet chocolate, such as Lindt,
  coarsely chopped
4 tablespoons unsalted butter, cut into small pieces
3 tablespoons sugar
$^1\!/_2$ cup all-purpose flour
2 large eggs
$1^1\!/_2$ teaspoon vanilla extract
$^1\!/_8$ teaspoon salt

Softened butter for the cupcake cups

Aluminum foil
Four 4-ounce aluminum cupcake cups (see headnote, page 130)

Grease the cupcake cups with softened butter.

Combine the chocolate and butter in the rice bowl (don't cover with foil), place the bowl in the steaming basket, cover, and steam until the chocolate is just melted, 10 to 12 minutes (see Equipment Notes). Remove the rice bowl from the steamer and stir in the sugar, flour, eggs, vanilla, and salt. Scrape down the sides and stir again to mix.

Scrape the chocolate mixture into the prepared cupcake cups and cover each with a square of aluminum foil. Place the cups in the steaming basket, cover, and steam until the sides are set but the center is still soft to the touch and gooey when pierced with a small knife, about 30 minutes.

Turn the cakes out onto individual plates and serve hot.

• **Equipment Notes:** The rice bowl in the Waring isn't large enough to hold all of the ingredients in the batter. Melt the chocolate with the butter in the solid-bottomed compartment, then scrape the mixture into a medium bowl and stir in the other ingredients until well mixed.

If using the Rival steamer, put the rice bowl directly on the steamer base, as described in the instruction manual, rather than in the steaming basket.

Coconut Rice Pudding

Serves 4
Water Level: High

This easy-to-make pudding pairs the satisfying chew of sweetened rice with velvety coconut-flavored vanilla custard. Use leftover cooked rice if you have it on hand, or steam three quarters of a cup raw white rice with one cup water according to the times on the chart on page 41.

$^1/_4$ **cup sweetened shredded coconut**
3 large eggs
$^1/_2$ **cup sugar**
1$^1/_2$ cups milk
$^1/_2$ **cup heavy cream**
1 teaspoon vanilla extract
$^1/_4$ **teaspoon salt**
2 cups cooked rice

Toast the coconut in a medium frying pan over medium heat, stirring occasionally, until golden brown, about 1 minute. Remove from the heat.

In a large bowl, whisk the eggs with the sugar until well mixed and light-colored. Add the coconut and the remaining ingredients, and stir to combine. Pour into the rice bowl and cover with aluminum foil. Place the rice bowl in the steaming basket (see Equipment Notes), cover, and steam until the custard is set but the center still jiggles slightly, about 35 minutes. Let cool, then refrigerate until chilled, 2 to 3 hours. Serve cold.

continued

• **Equipment Notes:** If using the Rival or Waring steamers, put the rice bowl directly on the steamer base, as described in the instruction manuals, rather than in the steaming basket.

Apple-Cinnamon Bread Pudding

Serves 6
Water Level: High

My experience with bread pudding is that it is often drier than it is pudding-like, and I end up using it as a sponge for added cream or ice cream. Because this pudding is steamed, it's moister than most. Use a dense bread such as Italian, or even sourdough.

This dessert can be served directly after steaming, but it's at its best cooled until firm (overnight in the refrigerator is fine), then sliced and toasted briefly in the oven.

**9 to 10 slices (3 to 4 inches square and about ½ inch thick) firm
   country-style white bread (see Note)**
2 cups milk (see Equipment Notes)
4 large eggs
⅓ cup plus ½ cup sugar
1 teaspoon vanilla extract
½ teaspoon cinnamon
3 tablespoons unsalted butter
3 Golden Delicious apples, peeled, cored, and sliced

Softened butter for the rice bowl

Aluminum foil

Preheat the oven to 400°F. Grease the rice bowl with softened butter.
    Put the bread slices on a baking sheet and toast in the oven until dry and starting to brown, about 15 minutes.

Meanwhile, scald the milk in a saucepan over medium-high heat. Remove from the heat.

In a large bowl, whisk the eggs with $\frac{1}{3}$ cup of the sugar until well mixed and light-colored. Gradually whisk in the warm milk and the vanilla.

Tear the bread into large pieces and add it to the egg mixture. Sprinkle the cinnamon over. Let soak for about 20 minutes, turning the bread occasionally so that it soaks evenly.

Melt the butter in a large frying pan over medium-high heat. Add the apples and the remaining $\frac{1}{2}$ cup sugar and cook, stirring frequently, until the apples have caramelized to a golden brown, about 15 minutes. Remove from the heat.

To assemble the pudding, layer half of the soaked bread in the prepared rice bowl. Cover with half of the apples. Repeat with the remaining bread and apples, and pour any egg mixture remaining in the bowl over all. Cover with aluminum foil, place in the steaming basket (see Equipment Notes), cover, and steam until the custard is just set, 45 to 50 minutes. Let cool for 1 to 2 hours, or let cool and then refrigerate overnight.

Preheat the oven to 450°F.

Run a knife around the edge of the pudding to loosen and then unmold it onto a plate. Cut the pudding into 1-inch slices and lay on a baking sheet. Toast in the oven until warmed through and lightly browned, 10 to 15 minutes. Serve hot.

• **Equipment Notes:** If using the Waring, cut the milk to $1\frac{3}{4}$ cups; 2 cups milk makes too much custard for the rice bowl, and the dessert won't be affected by using less milk.

If using the Rival or Waring steamers, put the rice bowl directly on the steamer base, as described in the instruction manuals, rather than in the steaming basket.

• **Note:** Fit the bread into the rice bowl before toasting to determine how many pieces you'll need.

Chocolate Bread Pudding

Serves 6

Water Level: High

I owe the inspiration for this dessert to one served by Anne Rozensweig at her restaurant, Arcadia, in New York City. It's divinely rich and buttery, best eaten warm.

You can serve it directly from the steamer; but, it is also very good made ahead, sliced, and toasted on a baking sheet for ten to fifteen minutes in a 450°F oven.

2 to 3 tablespoons unsalted butter, at room temperature
9 to 10 slices (3 to 4 inches square and about ¹/₂ inch thick) dense bread,
    such as Italian (see Note)
4 ounces good-quality bittersweet chocolate, such as Lindt,
    coarsely chopped
1 cup half-and-half
1 cup milk
2 large eggs
2 large egg yolks
¹/₄ cup sugar
¹/₂ teaspoon vanilla extract
Pinch of salt

Aluminum foil

Preheat the oven to 400°F.

Spread half the softened butter over one side of each slice of bread and place, buttered side down, on a baking sheet. Butter the other sides of the slices with the remaining butter and toast until golden brown, about 15 minutes. Set aside.

Combine the chocolate and ¹/₄ cup of the half-and-half in the rice bowl (don't cover with aluminum foil), place the rice bowl in the steaming basket (see Equipment Notes), cover, and steam until the chocolate melts, about 10 minutes.

Meanwhile, combine the remaining ¾ cup half-and-half and the milk in a medium saucepan and heat over medium heat until warm.

Gradually whisk the warm milk into the chocolate mixture.

In a medium bowl, combine the eggs, egg yolks, sugar, vanilla extract, and salt and whisk until well mixed and light-colored. Whisk in the chocolate mixture, and pour back into the rice bowl. Add the toasted bread slices to the bowl and let soak for 30 minutes, turning occasionally so that the bread soaks evenly.

Cover the rice bowl with aluminum foil, place it in the steaming basket, cover and steam for 50 minutes. Cut into slices and serve warm.

• **Equipment Notes:** If using the Rival or Waring steamers, put the rice bowl directly on the steamer base, as described in the instruction manuals, rather than in the steaming basket.

• **Note:** Fit the bread into the rice bowl before toasting to determine how many pieces you'll need.

Lemon Cheesecake

Serves 4

Water Level: Medium

Serve these individual cheesecakes plain with the sweetened sour cream and fresh raspberries, strawberries, and/or blueberries. Or serve with Fresh Blueberry Sauce (page 139).

GRAHAM CRACKER CRUST

$^{1}/_{4}$ cup graham cracker crumbs (2 crackers)

$2^{1}/_{4}$ teaspoons sugar

1 tablespoon unsalted butter, melted

LEMON FILLING

8 ounces cream cheese (preferably Fleur de Lait brand),
    at room temperature

$^{1}/_{4}$ cup sugar

1 large egg

$^{3}/_{4}$ teaspoon vanilla extract

Grated zest of 1 lemon

SWEETENED SOUR CREAM (OPTIONAL)

$^{1}/_{2}$ cup sour cream

1 tablespoon sugar

$^{1}/_{2}$ teaspoon vanilla extract

Softened butter for the cupcake cups

Parchment or waxed paper

Aluminum foil

Four 4-ounce aluminum cupcake cups (see headnote, page 130)

Grease the molds with softened butter. Line the bottoms of the molds with parchment paper or waxed paper rounds and butter the paper.

For the crust, stir all the ingredients together in a small bowl.

For the filling, in a medium bowl, beat the cream cheese and sugar with an electric mixer until creamy. Beat in the egg, vanilla, and lemon zest and beat until smooth (or mash the cream cheese and sugar together with a wooden spoon, then whisk in the remaining ingredients).

Pour the filling into the prepared molds and cover each with a square of aluminum foil. Place the molds in the steaming basket, cover, and steam until the cakes are completely set at the edges and a knife inserted into the centers comes out almost clean, 20 to 25 minutes. (Check each cake; some may steam faster than others.) Remove the cakes from the steamer and let cool. Then refrigerate until chilled, 1½ to 2 hours.

For the sweetened sour cream, if using, stir together the sour cream, sugar, and vanilla until well blended. Cover and refrigerate. (This can be made several hours ahead.)

To serve, turn the cheesecakes out onto individual plates and peel off the paper. Serve plain or with the sweetened sour cream, and berries if desired.

Fresh Blueberry Sauce

Serves 4

Water Level: Medium

½ **pint blueberries (about 1¼ cups)**
2 teaspoons fresh lemon juice
2 to 3 teaspoons sugar

Place the blueberries in the steaming basket, cover, and steam until soft, about 10 minutes. Press the berries through a fine strainer set over a bowl to puree. Stir in the lemon juice and 2 teaspoons sugar. Taste and add more sugar if needed. Chill and serve over ice cream or with Lemon Cheesecake (page138).

Peaches in Red Wine

Serves 4 to 6
Water Level: Medium
Preheat the Steamer

Traditionally, peaches, like tomatoes, are peeled by blanching them briefly in boiling water and then shocking them under cold running water; the skin pulls off easily after this treatment. Steaming gives the same result, without having to bring a large pot of water to the boil. This recipe is best made with sweet, ripe peaches. Don't overdo it—the idea is to steam only long enough to loosen the skin, not to cook the tender flesh.

The recipe calls for either strawberries or cherries to accompany the peaches. Use whichever look best—or use raspberries or blueberries if you prefer. If the fruit is ripe, a quarter cup of sugar should be enough; less-sweet fruit may need more sugar. If you use the cherries, be sure to warn your guests about the pits!

Serve this on its own or over ice cream or pound cake.

3 large ripe peaches (about 8 ounces each)
1 cup dry red wine
¼ cup sugar, or more if needed
1 pint strawberries, hulled and halved, or 2 cups stemmed cherries,
 with the pits

Preheat the steamer. Put the peaches in the steaming basket, cover, and steam until the skin detaches easily, 1 to 2 minutes. (The steaming time varies depending on how ripe the peaches are; very ripe peaches need very little time and will begin to cook and get mushy quickly.) Leaving the peaches in the steaming basket, refresh under cold running water. Drain well.

Pull the skin off the peaches. Stem the peaches and cut in half through the stem end. Gently twist the two halves of each peach to split the halves apart. Remove the pits and cut the peaches into quarters.

Combine the wine and sugar in a bowl. Add the peaches and strawberries or cherries and refrigerate until chilled, about 1 hour. Taste and add more sugar if needed.

Warm Brandied Bananas

Serves 2
Water Level: Medium

A simple recipe, this is easily varied by using another alcohol, such as rum, in place of the brandy; by adding a tablespoon of cream and/or grated chocolate, or the grated zest of a lemon, orange, or lime; or by sprinkling with toasted coconut, walnuts, or pecans just before serving. Serve the bananas on their own, with cookies, or over ice cream.

2 medium bananas, peeled and cut on the diagonal into
    1-inch-thick pieces
2 teaspoons sugar
2 teaspoons brandy
$\frac{1}{2}$ teaspoon vanilla extract
1 tablespoon unsalted butter, cut into pieces

Aluminum foil

Cut a 12- by 14-inch piece of aluminum foil and put the bananas in the center of the foil. Sprinkle with the sugar, drizzle the brandy and vanilla over, and dot with the butter. Bring two opposite sides of the foil up over the bananas and fold the edges together three times in $\frac{1}{4}$-inch folds to seal. Fold together the remaining sides in the same way. Place the foil package in the steaming basket and steam until just warmed through, about 10 minutes.

To serve, slit the foil open with a knife and slide the bananas onto individual plates. Drizzle the juices over and serve.

Steamed Pears with Warm Chocolate Sauce

Serves 2
Water Level: Medium

Unlike poaching, steaming doesn't add flavor to pears, so they must be ripe and sweet. Steamed pears have the best flavor if chilled.

2 ripe Anjou pears, peeled, halved, and cored

CHOCOLATE SAUCE

**4 ounces good-quality bittersweet chocolate, such as Lindt,
  coarsely chopped**
2 teaspoons water
1 teaspoon vanilla extract
2 tablespoons unsalted butter, cut into bits

4 sprigs fresh mint

Put the pears in a single layer in the steaming basket, cored sides down, cover, and steam until tender when pierced with a knife, about 20 minutes. Put the pears on a plate, cover, and refrigerate until chilled.

Just before serving, make the chocolate sauce: Put the chocolate and water in the rice bowl (don't cover with aluminum foil), put the rice bowl in the steaming basket (see Equipment Notes), cover, and steam until the chocolate melts, about 10 minutes. Remove the rice bowl from the steamer and whisk in the vanilla and butter.

To serve, set one pear half on each dessert plate. Spoon the warm chocolate sauce over and garnish each plate with a sprig of mint.

• **Equipment Notes:** If using the Rival or Waring steamers, put the rice bowl directly on the steamer base, as described in the instruction manuals, rather than in the steaming basket.

Apples with Rum and Fresh Ginger

Serves 2
Water Level: High

Serve these ginger-and-cinnamon-spiced apples hot or warm, with vanilla ice cream or heavy cream, if you like.

2 tablespoons raisins
1 tablespoon plus 1 teaspoon dark rum
2 Golden Delicious apples
1 tablespoon unsalted butter, at room temperature
$1/2$ teaspoon grated fresh ginger (see headnote, page 61)
$1/4$ teaspoon cinnamon
Pinch of salt

Aluminum foil

Put the raisins and 1 tablespoon of the rum in a small heatproof ramekin or custard cup and cover with a small square of aluminum foil. Place in the steaming basket, cover, and steam for 15 minutes, or until the raisins have absorbed most of the rum.

Meanwhile, peel the apples and core them with an apple corer or a small knife.

Mash together the butter, ginger, cinnamon, and salt. Gently stir in the raisins and any rum remaining in the ramekin or custard cup.

Cut two squares of aluminum foil large enough to wrap the apples loosely. Place an apple in the center of each piece of foil and stuff the apples with the raisin mixture. Sprinkle each apple with $1/2$ teaspoon rum. Bring the corners of the foil squares up to meet over the tops of the apples and press them together to seal. (Don't wrap the apples too tightly; there must be enough room in the foil packages for steam.)

Place the apples in the steaming basket, cover, and steam until the apples are tender, about 30 minutes.

To serve, slit open the foil with kitchen scissors or a knife and place each apple on an individual plate. Pour any juices over the apples and serve.

Chilled Apricots with Blueberries and Lime

Serves 2 to 3
Water Level: Medium

This easy, fat-free dessert is sweet and satisfying when apricots are in season, and the blue and orange of the two fruits are beautiful together. If the apricots are ripe, they dissolve a little in the sauce, thickening and sweetening it. The lime is surprisingly subtle and simply underlines the luscious fruitiness of the apricot. Serve this on its own or over ice cream—or with the end of a bottle of white wine or Champagne left from dinner poured over the fruit.

6 medium apricots
Juice of 1 lime
1 to 2 tablespoons sugar
1 cup blueberries

Cut the apricots in half through the stem end and pit them. Put the halves in the steaming basket cut sides down, cover, and steam until just tender, 12 to 15 minutes. Use a spatula or large spoon to transfer the apricots to a bowl and refrigerate until chilled, about 2 hours.

Add the lime juice, 1 tablespoon sugar, and the blueberries to the apricots, toss gently, and taste for sugar; add more if needed. Cover and let macerate in the refrigerator for 1 hour. Serve chilled.

Index